THE CONSOLATIONS
OF THEOLOGY

THE CONSOLATIONS
OF THEOLOGY

Edited by

Brian S. Rosner

William B. Eerdmans Publishing Company
Grand Rapids, Michigan / Cambridge, U.K.

Published 2008 by
Wm. B. Eerdmans Publishing Co.
2140 Oak Industrial Drive N.E., Grand Rapids, Michigan 49505 /
P.O. Box 163, Cambridge CB3 9PU U.K.
www.eerdmans.com

Printed in the United States of America

14 13 12 11 10 09 08   7 6 5 4 3 2 1

Library of Congress Cataloging-in-Publication Data

The consolations of theology / edited by Brian S. Rosner.
p.   cm.
Proceedings of a conference held in 2006 at
Moore Theological College, Sydney, Australia.
Includes bibliographical references.
ISBN 978-0-8028-6040-8 (pbk.: alk. paper)
1. Consolation — Congresses.   2. Theology — Congresses.
I. Rosner, Brian S.

BV4905.3.C66   2008
230 — dc22

2008004311

Contents

Preface

Theology, like philosophy, does not enjoy a reputation for keen relevance to everyday life. Practitioners of both disciplines pride themselves on their concern for ultimate truth and, rightly or wrongly, are thought to be averse to getting their hands dirty with the messiness of the human condition. When it comes to the knowledge of God, the famous stereotype is of monks debating how many angels can dance on the head of a pin!

In the modern era the Enlightenment insistence on the primacy of reason forced theology to pay little attention to the personal, the emotional, and the practical; but the tide does seem to be turning. The naïvety of neutral and dispassionate engagement with Scripture and Christian thought is now widely acknowledged. No one reads theology with indifference. And even if theologians prefer to talk in abstractions, a patient conversation with most of them reveals that their thinking about God has actually had a profound impact on their lives.

The great theologians in the history of the church have always found that theology affords genuine comfort in the face of life's difficulties. The majority did not live in cosseted ivory towers. To mention just three, Augustine was, to use modern terminology, a sex addict, Luther suffered from serious bouts of depression, and Bonhoeffer's life was marked by wretched tragedy. In such cases, heavenly thinking proved to be of earthly good.

Philosophy, too, has a long history of colorful characters with their own struggles whose thinking helped them to carry on. In recent years this has been demonstrated to great effect in the writings and documentaries of Alain de Botton. Most notably, his *Consolations of Philosophy* underscores the functional benefits of the most profound thinkers in the discipline.

In 2006, Moore Theological College in Sydney, Australia, where five of the contributors to this volume teach, hosted a conference on *The Consolations of Theology*. It was de Botton's similarly entitled book, and its practical philosophy, that inspired our own modest attempts to outline how theology affects our lives.

Digging around, it turned out that our decision to follow de Botton's *Consolations of Philosophy* with a *Consolations of Theology* is not without precedent. The first *Consolation of Philosophy*, by Boethius in the sixth century, was also adapted by Christians. Most notably, Jean Gerson and Thomas More each wrote a *Consolation of Theology*, in the fifteenth and sixteenth centuries respectively. Gwenfair Walters Adams tells this story in the Prologue of this book.

Just as Gerson and More adapted the basic genre of Boethius' pioneering work, we have followed the pattern of de Botton's book. In the present volume we ask what relief theology can offer to the perennial problems of life by looking not only to a major thinker's ideas but also to their own experience of hardship. The result is what we hope is a compelling blend of intriguing biography and profound theology and ethics addressing the range of human suffering. We are convinced that theology does indeed afford considerable comfort.

The consolations of theology are in the end the consolations of God. The apostle Paul expressed it well: like his, our ultimate aim is to introduce readers to "the God of all comfort, who comforts us in all our troubles, so that we can comfort those in any trouble with the comfort we ourselves have received from God" (2 Cor. 1:3-4).

BRIAN S. ROSNER

Prologue: On Consolation

Gwenfair Walters Adams

Some of the world's most powerful literature emerged in the nexus of enforced waiting, loneliness, deprivation, cold, hunger, and fear that has marked the arena, the dungeon, the tower, the jail. Over the centuries, many prisoners, when looking for comfort, turned to writing. One of the most famous of these prisoners was Anicius Manlius Severinus Boethius (A.D. 480-524). In the early sixth century, Boethius wrote a treatise on suffering that would become one of the most influential books of the next one thousand years.[1] It was *The Consolation of Philosophy.*

Critics credit Boethius with the invention of a new literary form, one combining in a fresh way many contemporary genres. It involved alternation between prose and poetry sections, used a dialogue between allegorical or typological figures who discussed complex ideas, and served a pedagogical purpose as the lead character learned and changed because of the progression of thought. Boethius also brought together the consolation and apocalyptic genres.[2]

In alternating poetry and prose, Boethius provided erudite entertain-

1. See Howard Rollin Patch, *The Tradition of Boethius: A Study of His Importance in Medieval Culture* (New York: Oxford University Press, 1935).

2. Michael H. Means, *The Consolatio Genre in Medieval English Literature,* University of Florida Humanities Monograph 36 (Gainesville, FL: University of Florida Press, 1972), pp. 7-9. See also Henry Chadwick, *Boethius: The Consolations of Music, Logic, Theology, and Philosophy* (New York: Oxford University Press, 1981), pp. 223-24, and Joel C. Relihan, *The Prisoner's Philosophy: Life and Death in Boethius's Consolation* (Notre Dame: University of Notre Dame Press, 2006).

ment so that he could explore complicated concepts without boring the reader. The poetry sections are often lyrical, replete with nature imagery. The prose parts are where the dialogue finds its home. The conversation is between Boethius and his visitor, Lady Philosophy. The Lady serves as a personification of the philosophy he has turned to for relief from the emotional pain of imprisonment and loss. Lady Philosophy leads Boethius from the easy answers of common platitudes to the harder answers of philosophical reasoning.[3] In the process, he is transformed from a depressed, despairing victim to a stalwart soldier.

Boethius' *Consolation* remained well known throughout the Middle Ages. It impacted dream-visions, prose dialogues, poetry, consolation literature, philosophy, views on reason and faith, theodicy, and scholasticism.[4]

In the fifteenth century, Jean Gerson, the famed Parisian theologian, finding himself in exile, took the opportunity to respond to his predecessor's book. He decided to imitate and adapt the structure of the prose and poetry alternation and also the dialogue. His dialogue took place between two imaginary characters, one of whom had supposedly just returned from visiting Gerson in his exile. The characters referred to Gerson as the *peregrino* or wayfarer. (Albrecht Dürer would later depict Gerson as a pilgrim in his famous engraving.) This exiled pilgrim sought to build on Boethius' work, intentionally building on to the consolations of philosophy those of theology. His work was therefore entitled *Consolation of Theology,* and it explored a number of themes of encouragement for those who needed comfort.[5]

A little over a hundred years later, another famous figure responded to Boethius' *Consolation of Philosophy* while he, too, was in prison: Thomas More, awaiting execution in the Tower of London. He wrote *The Dialogue of Comfort Against Tribulation,* and he also adapted Boethius' dialogue form. He, like Gerson, found philosophy to be insufficient in its consoling powers and turned to theology for comfort.[6]

3. Means, *The Consolatio Genre,* p. 9.

4. See Means, *The Consolatio Genre,* pp. 2-3; Chadwick, *Boethius,* pp. 252-53; and Boethius, *The Consolation of Philosophy,* trans. Richard Green (New York: Macmillan, 1962), pp. xxi, xxiii.

5. Jean Gerson, *The Consolation of Theology; De Consolatione Theologiae,* trans. Clyde Lee Miller (New York: Abaris Books, 1998), pp. v, 1-8.

6. *Thomas More: A Dialogue of Comfort against Tribulation,* ed. Frank Manley (New Haven: Yale University Press, 1976).

In 2000, Alain de Botton wrote his own *Consolations of Philosophy*. Although he did not imitate Boethius' dialogical or prose-poem sandwiching structure, he did follow him in inventiveness. He chose six philosophers and six topics. Then, weaving philosophical observations and instructions, an almost Monty Pythonesque use of illustrations, and lively writing, he offered consolations from Socrates for unpopularity, from Epicurus for not having enough money, from Seneca for frustration, from Montaigne for inadequacy, from Schopenhauer for a broken heart, and from Nietzsche for difficulties.[7]

The six authors in this book play off Alain de Botton's structure, choosing six figures and six topics, but they also follow Jean Gerson in his shift from philosophy to theology. Hence, the chapters in this book explore Lactantius on anger, Augustine on obsession, Luther on despair, Kierkegaard on anxiety, Bonhoeffer on disappointment, and C. S. Lewis on pain.

Boethius, Gerson, More, and de Botton all believed that the discussion of ideas could bring consolation. Our own conversation of consolation begins here.

---

7. Alain de Botton, *The Consolations of Philosophy* (New York: Random House, 2000).

LACTANTIUS

on Anger

RICHARD GIBSON

Be angry but do not sin; do not let the sun go down on your anger, and do not make room for the devil.

Ephesians 4:26-27

From God to Hero

Few moments in human history have been scrutinized as much as the 109th minute of the 2006 Football World Cup. A billion viewers around the world watched dumbfounded as the French captain, Zinedine Zidane, vigorously head-butted the Italian defender, Marco Materazzi, in the chest. Ejected from the field, Zidane seemed to have sacrificed both his team's chances of victory and his own glorious reputation, as "the greatest player of his generation." The commentator, Martin Tyler, summed it up almost instantly for his English-speaking audience: "You can make a reputation in fifteen years and lose it in fifteen seconds."

Zidane's "moment of madness" became a focus of world attention. Fans, commentators, politicians, even philosophers sought to explain it. Many maintained Tyler's initial verdict: "It doesn't matter what happened before — it doesn't justify retaliation." Besides, this was not the first time Zidane had been sent from the field for lashing out at an opponent. Others searched for mitigating circumstances. Materazzi must have provoked the attack. British tabloids hired lip-readers to translate Materazzi's jibes in the

1

lead-up to the incident. Rumors spread of appalling racial and personal slurs against Zidane's mother and sister. Zidane soon confirmed that Materazzi had used offensive language. Zidane had been deeply hurt: "I would rather have taken a punch in the face," he said, than hear such insults.[1] Some cashed in on the incident, with a head-butt song racing up the charts. Computer games soon followed. The rest of us simply took consolation from the fact we had finally seen someone do something at the World Cup that we were capable of.

In the days that followed, the incident took on the proportions of a Shakespearean tragedy, or better, one of Homer's epics. Some reluctantly demoted Zidane from the pantheon of "gods" to the rank of mere "hero." He was compared to Hercules who, despite his flaws, had made the world a better place by his conquests. One journalist likened Zidane to the French-Algerian character in a play by the existentialist Albert Camus. The character senselessly shoots an Arab on the beach. Helpfully, the journalist clarified that Zidane

> did not kill anyone in the glare of the floodlights of Berlin's Olympic Stadium. His senseless act, beneath the gaze of a billion people, merely knocked an Italian off his feet. All that Zidane killed was a certain narrative of his life.[2]

The narrative of Zidane had read like this: From the poverty of his childhood as the son of Algerian immigrants, Zidane rose to be the superstar of the world game. He was a model for those in similar circumstances and a symbol of hope that France might rise above her shameful history of treatment of her Algerian immigrant population. But had this moment of thuggery and his history of violence merely shown that he could not finally emerge from that environment? The right-wing Italian Senate President, Roberto Calderoli, thought so. He claimed that the French team "sacrificed its identity by selecting blacks, Islamists, and communists." If you select barbarians, you have to expect them to act like barbarians. In re-

---

1. Susan Sachs, "To the French, Zidane still a hero, if no longer a 'god,'" *Christian Science Monitor* July 14, 2006. Cited 10 September 2006. Online: http://www.csmonitor.com/2006/0714/p01s01-woeu.html.

2. Roger Cohen, "Camus and Zidane," *DeccanHerald* July 13, 2006. Cited 10 September 2006. Online: http://www.deccanherald.com/deccanherald/jul132006/panorama1742332006712.asp.

sponse, one French philosopher came to Zidane's defense. François Sureau could see a way to resurrect the narrative: "I see, thanks to Zidane, the victory of a certain national spirit." Zidane, Sureau said, "has given us back our beautiful reputation for insolence."[3]

Analyzing Anger

The moment and its aftermath became a fascinating case study in anger — its causes, appropriateness, and consequences. The spectrum of opinion raised a range of questions. Was his anger simply irrational and inexplicable? Was it understandable, but inexcusable? Does some kind of provocation mitigate, or even justify, anger? Does some provocation even demand anger and vengeance? Is the crucial issue really the retaliation? Would anyone notice the 109th minute if Zidane fumed angrily but did not act? Was this a moment of shame, exposing a petty and violent soul? Or a moment for pride, when the nobility of one man's spirit transcended sport and defended the honor of family and country, at great personal cost? Do gods get angry? Do they cease to be gods if they do?

If there is any consolation at this early stage, it is that our moments of anger and vengefulness are not subject to such public analysis. None of us would want a billion people watching archival footage of our angriest moments, unless we had a French philosopher as our advocate. Many of us can readily identify with Zidane's moment. We know the spiral. Incensed by an insult or perceived slight; the seething feeling of resentment; the rash act, perhaps words of murderous intent or the impulsive physical act; the proud defiance; the hopeless despair at not being able to undo it; the gradual realization of the damage to relationship, trust, credibility; the desperate attempts to explain, to rationalize; the search for someone to blame; and the shame that sticks to your soul like chewing gum to your shoe. We know what it is like to feel a certain narrative of our life die: the exemplary leader, the loving parent, the faithful friend, the laid-back, got-it-all-together, mature Christian person.

Many of us blush at the recollection of bitter exchanges with colleagues at work who don't see things our way, of rage at the motorist who is slow to move off when the lights turn green, of pitched verbal battles

3. Sachs, "To the French."

3

with partners after a demoralizing day, of vengeful words behind the back of a friend who disappointed us; or of the settled malice that still lingers from unresolved conflict. In our self-recrimination we would gladly book in for the operation to have the capacity for anger surgically removed from our breast, or spleen, or bile duct. Yet, is that necessary or wise? There are other times when we can't shake the conviction that our anger is righteous, that an injustice ought to be exposed, that our angry opposition to corruption and evil is a noble, even godly, quality.

The Consolation of Theology

The real consolation I hope to offer in this chapter is from theology: to explore how setting the question of anger in the context of Christian theology sharpens our questions, construes our struggles, and shines light into our confusion. More particularly, I want to focus these questions through the lens of a particular Christian writer, Lactantius. Lactantius would regard our struggle with anger as a worthy topic of reflection. His writings reveal a special interest in, and concern for, the phenomenon of anger in human relationships and in God's relationship to the world. In contrast to much of his philosophical and theological heritage, Lactantius regarded anger as essential to human existence and God's providential care of the world.

Furthermore, Lactantius would have recognized Zidane's head-butt as a classic example of a moment fueled by anger. Like most thinkers in the ancient world, his understanding of anger was shaped by Aristotle's seminal definition. According to Aristotle, anger is

> a longing (ὄρεξις), accompanied by pain (λύπης), for a real or apparent revenge for a real or apparent slight, affecting a man himself or one of his friends, when such a slight is undeserved.[4]

Importantly, a definition like this opens up the possibility of analysis and reflection. If anger is simply an irrational, reflex-like response, then there is little to be gained by examination. Aristotle's definition gives us some

---

4. Aristotle, *Rhetoric* 2.2. Diogenes Laertius, 7.113, provides a standard Stoic definition along these lines for ὀργή: "a craving or desire to punish one who is thought to have done you an undeserved injury."

questions with which to interrogate and evaluate a moment of anger. It leaves open the possibility that anger is warranted. While Lactantius does understand anger in these terms, he will modify the definition, precisely because of the theological perspective he brings to the subject. To appreciate this, we need to understand the wider context of Lactantius' approach.

Lactantius, the "Not Quite a Theologian"

The remains of history only allow a line-drawing of the life of L. Caecilius Firmianus Lactantius.[5] Had he attended the 2006 World Cup final he probably would have identified with Zidane.[6] Like Zidane he had his roots in Africa and rose to prominence in Gaul. He was born about A.D. 250 into a pagan family in North Africa, where he studied rhetoric under Arnobius the Elder. Though he trained many advocates and jurists, he admits that he lacked the eloquence required to enter public life as a career lawyer.[7] Yet, Emperor Diocletian appointed him as teacher of rhetoric in Nicomedia. Somewhere very early in the fourth century he converted to Christianity. Soon after, he was forced to resign from his position in the face of the persecution of 303, which denied Christians any official posts. It was during this period that he produced his writings on a variety of subjects. Later he enjoyed the favor of Emperor Constantine, serving as tutor to his son Crispus at the imperial court at Trier in Gaul, from about 317. He died about a decade later. So, had he been in the crowd at the Berlin Stadium he would have most likely supported France. It is much more likely that he would not buy tickets to the match and refuse them if they were offered to him. Lactantius writes scathingly of the entertainment of his day, especially the games; because they "offer great incitement to vice and are very powerful in corrupting the soul, we must abolish

5. Even his name is disputed, some insisting on Caelius. Lactantius, *Divine Institutes*, trans. with intro. and notes by A. Bowen and P. Garnsey (Liverpool: Liverpool University Press, 2003), p. 1.

6. Claims that his name suggests Italian origins have proven unconvincing. See Pierre de Labriolle, *History and Literature of Christianity from Tertullian to Boethius*, trans. H. Wilson (London: Routledge & Kegan Paul, 1924; 1968), p. 200: "From St Jerome's notice of him . . . we may conclude that he was an African." Labriolle provides one of the best introductions to Lactantius' writings.

7. Lactantius, *Inst.* 3.13.12.

them. They don't just have nothing to give to the life of bliss, they actually do it great damage."[8]

Lactantius is pointedly remembered as a rhetorician and apologist. Nearly everyone who writes about Lactantius feels obliged to point out his intellectual limitations and failure to warrant the title of "theologian."[9] It is an assessment that can be traced back to Jerome, writing nearly two centuries after Lactantius, and is repeated by most scholarly treatments.[10] Descriptions include: "not an intelligence of the first order";[11] "As a theologian, he does not count. He is a far from trustworthy exponent, and some of his interpretations are wholly lacking in taste"; "possessed of an intelligence of no very great compass."[12] "Even when we exert ourselves to say something good of him it would be puerile to endeavour to cover up the weaknesses in the train of thought of this conscientious professor."[13] My personal favorite: "mediocre, 'in the Latin sense of the word, — and a little also in the French sense.'"[14] All of these slurs are derived from one source: a chapter of less than twenty pages by Pierre Labriolle. One cannot help suspecting that this final slur was the one with which Materazzi pushed Zidane over the brink: "O Zinedine, you are mediocre, in the Latin sense of the word, and a little also in the French sense."

These perceptions of Lactantius warn against expecting too much from him. He does not ask all our questions about anger, let alone answer them. Some of his answers will not satisfy. Yet the danger of rehearsing these scholarly assessments is the prejudice they might promote against

---

8. Lactantius, *Inst.* 6.20.9 [Bowen & Garnsey].

9. M. P. McHugh, "Lactantius," in *Encyclopaedia of Early Christianity* 2nd ed., ed. E. Ferguson (New York: Garland, 1998), p. 660, "Christian Latin apologist . . . A rhetorician and not a theologian." Johannes Quasten, *Patrology: Volume 2 The Ante-Nicene Literature after Irenaeus* (Utrecht-Antwerp: Spectrum, 1964), pp. 405-6, "he is not a genuine theologian; he lacks both the knowledge and the capacity." Marcia L. Colish, *The Stoic Tradition from Antiquity to the Early Middle Ages: 2. Stoicism in Christian Latin thought through the Sixth Century* (Leiden: Brill, 1990), p. 40: "Lactantius has frequently been described as an intellectual bantamweight, lacking a profound or speculative mind. He is typically treated as an eclectic whose understanding of philosophy was shallow and use of it was strictly *ad hoc.*"

10. Jerome, *Epilogue* 58.10.

11. Labriolle, *History and Literature*, p. 199. This is one of the best introductions to Lactantius' thought.

12. Labriolle, *History and Literature*, p. 207.

13. Labriolle. *History and Literature*, p. 200.

14. Labriolle. *History and Literature*, p. 199.

what Lactantius does contribute. Lactantius has much to offer on the subject of anger, exploring possibilities rejected by some of the luminaries of Christian theology who supposedly dwarf him. In fairness, very few Latin writers of the first five centuries, apart from Tertullian and Augustine, shine with the luster of the more philosophically inclined theologians of the East. My hope is that limited, shallow, and mediocre intellects are capable of deriving consolation from theology.

We should not underestimate Lactantius. Labriolle also points to some of the reasons that Lactantius was ranked so highly by humanists of the Renaissance, and continues to attract so much interest from contemporary French, German, and Italian commentators (much more than English-speaking). The humanists referred to him as "the Christian Cicero," for the purity of his literary style.[15] Labriolle also admits that "each time he touches upon moral questions, he interests and almost moves us," adding, "we meet with fine intuitions, and all the *clairvoyances* of a delicate soul which really feels the truth of Christianity and which knows how to make it appeal to the heart." Having noted that no one before him had better differentiated Christianity and paganism, Labriolle adds admiringly, "in places Lactantius reached the real foundation of the Christian spirit."[16]

Others offer more substantial appreciation. According to Bowen and Garnsey, Lactantius "fashioned a kind of Christian apologetic that had never been seen before." "A proper assessment of Lactantius," they argue, "would highlight his singular achievement in constructing a coherent body of Christian ethical thinking, against the background of and in critical dialogue with classical thought."[17] His were shoulders on which Augustine would stand.[18] There is also a growing appreciation of his significance for the earliest history of Christendom. He was the first Latin Christian author under Constantine's rule.[19] One recent study argues that

15. McHugh, "Lactantius," p. 660. Cf. the frank assessment of Quasten, *Patrology,* pp. 393-94, "Unfortunately, the quality of his thought does not correspond to the excellence of its expression. Most of his work is compilation and evinces shallowness and superficiality."

16. Labriolle, *History and Literature,* pp. 207, 209.

17. Bowen and Garnsey, *Divine Institutes,* p. 1.

18. Peter Garnsey, "Lactantius and Augustine," *Proceedings of the British Academy* 114 (2002): 175-76.

19. Oliver Nicholson, "Arnobius and Lactantius," in *The Cambridge History of Early Christian Literature,* ed. F. Young, L. Ayres, and A. Louth (Cambridge: Cambridge University

Lactantius exercised considerable influence on Constantine's religious policy, playing a determinative role in the constitution of the emerging Christian Empire.[20]

Lactantius' Audience and Method

There are other features of Lactantius' writings that a modern evangelical reader needs to be prepared for. Lactantius was determined to reach sophisticated unbelievers. His education and work led him to highly value erudition. Lactantius felt acutely the contempt for Christianity among the cultured elite. He mentions the anti-Christian writings of a particular philosopher and a judge, unable to decide whether they are driven by disdain or perversity.[21] At the beginning of his major work, *Divine Institutes,* Lactantius explains his hope to apply his learning in commending the Christian faith, and thus offer a more expert defense than Christians had been able to supply:

> Though truth can be defended, as many have often defended it, without eloquence, nevertheless it ought to be illuminated and indeed maintained with clarity and splendour of utterance, so that it floods into people's minds more forcefully, with the equipment of its own power and religion and its own brilliance of rhetoric.[22]

In his treatise on *The Anger of God,* he describes three steps that any unbeliever must be guided through. First, they have to be persuaded of the falseness and vanity of alternative gods. Second, they need to be con-

---

Press, 2004), p. 265: "If we are to understand the sort of Christianity to which Constantine the Great was converted, it is to Lactantius that we must turn."

20. E. D. Digeser, *The Making of a Christian Empire: Lactantius and Rome* (Ithaca, N.Y.: Cornell University Press, 2000), p. 138, "A close comparison of Lactantius' and Constantine's writings thus suggests that a Christian doctrine of concord, one that grew out of a theory of toleration invented to stem violence against Christians, became imperial policy in an effort to control Christian aggression . . . It also demonstrates that Lactantius' theology was a useful point of reference for the first Christian emperor. And finally it suggests that the *Divine Institutes* may hold a key to other puzzling aspects of this emperor's still hotly debated religious policy."

21. Lactantius, *Inst.* 5.2.

22. Lactantius, *Inst.* 1.1.10 [Bowen and Garnsey]; 5.2.1.

vinced of the existence of the one true, living God. These phases equipped
the enquirer

> to know His Servant and Messenger, whom He sent as His ambassador
> to earth, by whose teaching being freed from the error in which we were
> held entangled, and formed to the worship of the true God, we might
> learn righteousness.[23]

His more extensive and systematic treatment of the faith, the *Divine Institutes*, clearly follows this pattern.

Perhaps the most disconcerting feature of Lactantius' writings is his
avoidance of explicit argumentation from biblical texts. Apart from the
section of *Divine Institutes* discussing the incarnation and supporting
proofs from Old Testament prophecy, invocation of Scripture is negligible.[24] Lactantius criticizes Cyprian for relying on biblical texts. While the
Bible is perfectly useful for Christians, unbelievers could not be expected
to accept arguments from literature they regarded vain, fictitious, inferior,
contradictory, and novel.[25] Lactantius is much more likely to appeal to
Virgil, Cicero, Seneca, or even the Sibylline Oracles and writings of Hermes Trismegistos. This data could easily misrepresent Lactantius, however.
It is true that he judged much Scripture as lacking in literary style. More
importantly, his apologetic strategy dictated that it is more persuasive to
establish common ground with arguments a pagan audience might count
as valid. Part of his criticism of Cyprian was that he did not speak in a way
that communicated to a non-Christian audience.[26]

At the same time, Lactantius remains "a theologian of revelation,"
convinced that philosophy offers no true knowledge of God.[27] He rejects
as arrogant any suggestion that "truth is comprehended by our intellect."
Rather, Christians "follow the teaching of God, who alone is able to know
and reveal secret things." Philosophical speculation offers no consolation
at all, since the human mind "enclosed in the dark abode of the body, is far

23. Lactantius, *On the Wrath of God* 2, in *Lactantius: The Minor Works*, trans. M. F. Mc-
Donald (Washington, D.C.: Catholic University of America Press, 1965).

24. Lactantius, *Inst.* 4.5.3: "Their evidence is now relevant. In my earlier books I held
off."

25. Lactantius, *Inst.* 4.5.9-10; 5.2.13-16. Labriolle, *History and Literature*, p. 204.

26. H. von Campenhausen, *The Fathers of the Latin Church*, trans. M. Hoffmann (London: A. & C. Black, 1964), p. 64.

27. Campenhausen, *Fathers*, p. 70.

removed from the perception of truth."[28] It is frequently apparent that whole discussions are informed by Scriptural texts, even though they are not made explicit. An imperfect analogy to Lactantius' approach might be sought in Paul's speech to the Areopagus (Acts 17:22-34). There, Paul argues with his educated and skeptical audience using language and literary sources familiar to them, though the content of his speech is profoundly informed by his biblical theology.[29]

Angry Lactantius?

The sketchiness of the biographical data means we have little indication of Lactantius' own struggle with the emotion, anger. Was he prone to anger, possessed of a choleric temperament? We do not know. What made him angry? We do not know. We can only speculate from his literary remains. To Campenhausen, the "cultivated and well-balanced manner" of his writings reveals "his genuine, unobtrusive, cool and restrained nature."[30] However, there is evidence for a contrary mirror reading based on the content of his writings.[31] They reflect his persistent interest and radical conclusions about anger. Human anger is discussed at various points in *Divine Institutes,* written between 305 and 310, and consequently in its digest form, the *Epitome* (317). The *Institutes* (2.17) raises the issue of God's anger, but promises another treatise due to the sheer amount of information. His treatise *On the Anger of God* was produced in 313 or the following year. About a year later, Lactantius wrote *The Deaths of the Persecutors,* an exposition of how God's anger had been visited on all those emperors who had persecuted Christians.[32]

If this interest does reflect an acquaintance with anger, what might have

---

28. Lactantius, *Wrath of God* 1 [McDonald].

29. R. J. Gibson, "Paul and the Evangelization of the Stoics," in *The Gospel to the Nations: Perspectives on Paul's Mission. Essays in Honour of Peter Thomas O'Brien,* ed. P. G. Bolt and M. D. Thompson (Leicester: InterVarsity Press, 2000), pp. 309-26.

30. Campenhausen, *Fathers,* p. 64.

31. Hans Lietzmann, *A History of the Early Church Volume 2* (Cambridge: James Clarke, 1993), p. 720, comments regarding his attitude toward the end of the world: "It shows that he was no mere cool rational thinker as he had seemed. The terrors of the times of persecution still reverberated in his heart, and laid his soul open to accept ideas born of an unlimited yearning for a bright future not of this world."

32. For these dates, McHugh, "Lactantius," p. 660.

triggered it? Three possibilities emerge: poverty, persecution, and philosophy. According to Jerome, Lactantius was "a pauper in this life as he generally lacked even the necessities."[33] Even in his official capacity in Nicomedia, he was driven to writing by a lack of Latin students. In a Greek city only public servants would need Latin. By the time Diocletian launched his ferocious persecution of Christians, especially in the East of the empire, Lactantius was converted. While he avoided physical torture, he was forced to leave his job and take refuge, with no apparent means of support.

Whether or not the personal impact of the "Great Persecution" was a source of irritation and resentment, the treatment of fellow Christians seems to have provoked a passionate response. This is his commentary on a set of regulations prescribing penalties for Christians:

> What are you to do with people who call it law when elderly tyrants turn butcher and go rabid against the innocent? They are teachers of injustice and cruelty, and yet they want to seem just and wise when they are blind and stupid, and ignorant of facts and truth. Is justice something you hate so much, you poor lunatics, that you set it on a par with the greatest of crimes? Is innocence so dead among you that you think it undeserving of even a simple death, and that confessing to no crime and presenting a soul clean of all contagion is to be counted the crime above all crimes?[34]

It is easy to imagine a vindictive motivation behind *The Deaths of the Persecutors,* a historical piece that relishes the miserable deaths suffered by persecuting emperors. "The glorification of the bloody martyrdoms," says Campenhausen, "has a repulsive effect, and the merciless triumph over the cruelly overthrown enemies of Christianity is rather offensive."[35] If Lactantius' relief and joy under Constantine's benevolent rule are the obverse of his anger against previous persecuting regimes, then it was deeply felt. As Walsh aptly and more sympathetically expresses it, Lactantius speaks on behalf of a church "which knows the elevation and excitement of feeling that come from the sense of being in the care of a jealous God."[36]

---

33. Jerome, *Chronicle,* pp. 310-11.

34. Lactantius, *Inst.* 5.12.1 [Bowen and Garnsey].

35. Campenhausen, *The Fathers,* p. 82.

36. William J. Walsh, "The Image of the Church in Lactantius' *De Mortibus Persecutorum*" in *Kyriakon: Festschrift Johannes Quasten. Volume 2* (2 vols.), ed. P. Granfield and J. A. Jungmann (Münster: Verlag Aschendorff, 1970), p. 526.

Behold, all our adversaries are crushed; tranquility is restored throughout the world; the Church, but recently buffeted by persecution, now
rises again; and the temple of God, which had been overturned by the
impious, is rebuilt in greater splendour by the mercy of the Lord . . . the
cloud of that most bitter period having been dissolved, so to speak, a
joyous and serene peace rejoices the hearts of all men. Now, after the
violent whirlwinds of a dark storm, a clear sky with longed-for light
has shown forth . . . He has dried the tears of those who mourned . . .
those who hacked the just to pieces have poured forth their lives that
wrought harm, punished by blows sent from heaven and well-deserved
tortures.[37]

At least one commentator detects some bitter resentment in Lactantius' in-
teraction with philosophers. According to Labriolle, the "scholarly art and
the cruelly skillful arguments" of one of his opponents "had inflamed him
with an ardent desire to refute them, and with them, all those who either in
Greek or Latin had accomplished the same detestable task."[38] Labriolle
sees a connection with the persecutions at this point. "Echoes of the persecution still rumble" in the *Divine Institutes,* and during this period certain
philosophers had been implacable in their opposition to Christianity.
Consequently, Labriolle reckons Lactantius "has little love for the philosophers," and "treats them very harshly": their arbitrary constructions and
hypocritical lifestyles "irritate him" into delivering a fierce attack.[39]

On Human Anger

While they betray little regarding the sources of Lactantius' anger, his writings contribute richly on the topic. According to Lactantius, there are three
primary passions, or to use the poets' term, three "furies." Anger wants revenge; love of gain wants wealth; and sexual desire wants pleasure.[40] These

37. Lactantius, *The Deaths of the Persecutors* 1, in *The Minor Works,* trans. M. F. McDon-
ald (Washington, D.C.: Catholic University of America Press, 1965), pp. 137-38.
38. Labriolle, *History and Literature,* p. 203.
39. Labriolle, *History and Literature,* p. 205.
40. Lactantius, *Epitome* p. 61. In adopting this triad Lactantius follows Cicero (*Tusc.*
3.25), Virgil, and Horace. The Stoics, like Seneca, recognized four primary passions: pleasure,
desire, fear, and grief.

are strong impulses, which excite people's minds. In doing so, they are capable of wreaking great havoc on society. Yet they are intended and necessary for the maintenance of life. Without sexual desire the species would die out. Without a desire for gain, people would fail to provide for themselves and their families. Without anger, evil would remain unchecked. According to Lactantius, the emotion of anger "is the condition of the survival of society, inasmuch as no political power can stand without it, or the fear that naturally accompanies it."[41] Consequently, the challenge is to restrain them. The key here is not their removal or diminution, but their expression within the boundaries for which they were intended. Outside these boundaries, sexual desire drives us to adultery and debauchery; love of gain to poisoning, false wills, and fraud; anger to cruelty, slaughters, and war. Outside these boundaries the three become diseases of the soul and vicious. By keeping them within proper bounds and directing them to their intended goals, we prove to be "patient, brave, and just."[42]

Lactantius hammers out the place of this triad in conversation with the Peripatetics (philosophic heirs of Aristotle) and the Stoics. The Stoics insist on their eradication because they regard all emotions as sicknesses of the mind. Lactantius thinks they are "mad" for wanting "in some fashion to castrate people" of these impulses.[43] He agrees with the Peripatetics that these impulses are innate; we have them from birth. More importantly, he believes they were implanted in us by God, with his good purposes in mind. In fact, there is something wrong with the person who does not lust for their marriage partner, covet the needs of their family, or feel anger at their child's misbehavior.

The Peripatetics advocated moderation, finding the appropriate mean for any situation. While Lactantius shares more common ground with the Peripatetics, they, too, err in their approach to these emotions. It is not a matter of striking some ideal median or balance. If an emotion is evil then it should not just be restrained, but eliminated. Envy provides the best example of an emotion condemned in philosophical and biblical treatments.[44] However, "if they are good, we ought to use them in their completeness." As good gifts from God, we ought to allow ourselves to be ex-

---

41. Gábor Kendeffy, "Lactantius on the Passions," *Acta Classica Universitatis Scientarum Debreceniensis* 36 (2000): 114.

42. Lactantius, *Inst.* 6.19.1-10; *Epitome* 61.

43. Lactantius, *Inst.* 6.15.3.

44. Lactantius, *Wrath of God* 16.

cited in these ways. Thus Lactantius concludes: "These passions, therefore, must be kept within their boundaries and directed into their right course, in which, even though they should be vehement, they cannot incur blame."[45] This object orientation is central to Lactantius' perspective:

> As I said, wisdom is not concerned with control of these feelings but in control of what causes them, because emotions are stirred from the outside, and putting curbs on them is particularly inappropriate since they are capable of being slight where there is much wrong and of being huge where there is nothing wrong; they should have been related to particular times, circumstances and places, in case feelings which one may correctly exercise become vices. It is good to walk straight and bad to go astray; so too it is good to be emotionally moved in the right direction, and bad in the wrong direction.[46]

The implication of our created natures is that each of us faces the struggle to be excited in the right way, directing our emotions toward God's intended goals. This struggle is also part of God's good intentions for us, because the struggle trains us in virtue. In this sense, the Stoics deny people the opportunity to practice virtue by denying them the emotion of anger. It is precisely in the regulation of its impulsive character that we grow. Lactantius' image for this task is the cultivation of a fertile field. Each of us is called to be a soul-gardener:

> Emotions are a sort of natural exuberance of souls: fields which are naturally fertile grow a wealth of brambles, and in the same way any untilled soul chokes itself with vices that flourish like thorns. When the true farmer comes, however, at once the vices give way and the fruits of virtue spring up.
> When God first made man, with marvellous foresight he bred in him first the sort of feelings which would enable him to acquire virtue as a land gets cultivation, and he planted the stuff of vice in the emotions and the stuff of virtue in the vices.[47]

The tendency of anger to destructive, anti-social behavior is never lost on Lactantius. In human relationships, anger needs to be curbed. Our an-

45. Lactantius, *Epitome* 61.
46. Lactantius, *Inst.* 6.16.7-8 [Bowen and Garnsey].
47. Lactantius, *Inst.* 6.15.8-9 [Bowen and Garnsey].

ger is often unjust. It is usually an immediate emotion, flaring up for a time at some irritation or provocation. Unless moderated it can drive people to disproportionate responses and terrible crimes (*Ira* 21). This tendency means the tightest strictures must be placed on its expression. It is never something to be directed to those in authority over us nor toward those who are our peers or equals. When people "vent anger on their equals" the result is division and alienation, and "the wars that rise against injustice."[48]

Instead, anger has its place in the discipline of those in our care or under our authority, for instance in the discipline of children.

> It is both just and necessary to use anger against the young; . . . The reason I have given for man having the emotion of anger can be seen in the precepts of God himself: he says we should not be angry with those who attack us, verbally or otherwise, but we should always have the upper hand over the young, in order to correct them with instant beatings when they sin, so that futile affection and over indulgence do not rear them to evil and fatten them up for vice.[49]

To a culture currently discussing the merits of smacking children these words are confronting. It ought to be recognized that the passage consciously echoes the language of Hebrews 12:4-12, a passage about God's discipline of his children. In an earlier section of the *Institutes*, Lactantius discusses the kindness of God's discipline "in not permitting our corruption to proceed any further, putting us right with blows and beatings." Characteristically, Lactantius cites Seneca's *On Providence*, rather than Hebrews.[50]

Lactantius' curiously hierarchical discussion reflects his wrestling with Matthew 5. It was Jesus himself who placed the strictest controls on the human expression of anger, and drives Lactantius to define very carefully where anger is to be expressed:

> But I say to you that if you are angry with a brother or sister, you will be liable to judgment; and if you insult a brother or sister, you will be liable to the council; and if you say, "You fool," you will be liable to the hell of fire. (Matt. 5:22)

48. Lactantius, *Inst.* 6.19.10.
49. Lactantius, *Inst.* 6.19.7-9 [Bowen and Garnsey].
50. Lactantius, *Inst.* 5.22.12-13.

This crucial text reads very much like an absolute prohibition of anger, the kind of call to uncompromising elimination found frequently in Epicurean and Stoic writings, and lent authority by other biblical texts. This one comes with the authority of Jesus himself. However, for reasons we are about to discuss, Lactantius refuses to read this as an absolutist prohibition of anger.

On God's Anger

Much of Lactantius' treatment of the topic reads as a conversation between Matthew 5 and Ephesians 4:26-27. He responds to those who claim that God's prohibition of anger reveals its incompatibility with God's nature. But if this were the case God would be censuring his own workmanship. From the beginning "he inserted anger in the liver of man."[51] In fact, God commands us to be angry. Here, Ephesians 4:26, though not explicitly cited, comes clearly into view: "Be angry (ὀργίζεσθε) but do not sin." From this, Lactantius draws the inference that:

> since He has commanded man to be angry, indeed, and yet not to sin, certainly He did not tear out anger by its roots, but He tempered it, so that in all chastisement we might hold to measure and justice. (*Wrath of God* 21 [Donaldson])

To those familiar with the NIV rendering of these verses, Lactantius' reading will seem strained. "In your anger do not sin" hardly reads as a command to be angry. However, the Greek can certainly be read in the way Lactantius maintains. Wallace's exegesis of Ephesians 4:26-27 supports the suggestion that we are commanded to be angry at sin in order to drive it out of our churches. In fact, attempts to soften the imperatival mood of the first part of verse 26, argues Wallace, do not stand up to grammatical scrutiny. Wallace also questions the usual rendering of the second imperative in verse 26: "Do not let the sun go down while you are still angry" (NIV). For Lactantius, this prohibits perseverance in anger. Our anger is to be mortal, or short-lived. Wallace points out that the noun παροργισμός is more likely to mean the "cause of your anger,"

---

51. Lactantius, *Wrath of God* 21.

rather than the emotion experienced, as most English versions render it.[52] Wallace concludes, "both imperatives should be taken at face value." On this reconstruction, verse 27

> would thus mean that one should not give a place to the devil *by doing nothing about the sin in the midst of the believing community.* Entirely opposite to the "introspective conscience" view, this text seems to be a shorthand expression for church discipline, suggesting that there is biblical warrant for δικαία οργή (as the Greeks put it) — righteous indignation.

To some extent this understanding harmonizes with Matthew 5, where Jesus insists we are to deal with provocations quickly and seek reconciliation.

In construing the text as Paul's insistence on short-lived anger, Lactantius perceives a connection between God's anger and ours. "His rejection of *apatheia* as an acceptable moral state for man," observes Colish, "is closely related to his rejection of *apatheia* as an adequate description of God."[53] Lactantius concludes from Ephesians 4:

> Therefore He who commands us to be angry is manifestly Himself angry; He who enjoins us to be quickly appeased is manifestly Himself easy to be appeased: for He has enjoined those things which are just and useful for the interests of society. (*Wrath of God* 21)

Lactantius is fully aware of the controversial nature of this reasoning. He runs the risk, to refined, pagan ears, of depicting God like the gods of mythology. The possibility of God being angry had been repudiated by philosophers like Cicero and Seneca, and by theologians like Clement, Origen, and his teacher Arnobius. Lactantius is aware that the claim requires some qualification. There are some emotions that are unworthy of God: fear, avarice, grief, and envy. God's anger is never "inflamed with an immediate excitement" like ours, because God is "eternal and of perfect virtue, and He is never angry unless deservedly." God always controls his anger, is never ruled by it, regulates it according to his will. This leads to a tension

---

52. Daniel B. Wallace, *Greek Grammar Beyond the Basics,* (Grand Rapids: Zondervan, 1996), p. 492. Cf. 1 Kings 15:30; 2 Kings 23:26; Neh. 9:18; Ps. Sol. 8:8-9. For an extended discussion of the options and exegetical issues, see Wallace, "Ὀργίζεσθε in Ephesians 4:26: Command or Condition?" *Criswell Theological Review* (1989): 352-72.

53. Colish, *Stoic Tradition,* p. 46.

felt by Lactantius. In contrasting divine and human anger, he describes God's anger as eternal. It ever remains against those who persevere in sin. Yet, the God who commands us to seek reconciliation before sunset is appeased by those who repent: the person "who ceases to sin renders the anger of God mortal" (*Ira* 21).

In maintaining the reality of God's anger, Lactantius' conversation partners are the Epicurean and Stoic schools. In responding to their positions, he analyzes the relationship between God's anger and kindness *(beneficentia)*, or grace *(gratia)*. He outlines four possible permutations. Logically, God may be subject to neither anger nor kindness. Or, God could be kind but not given to anger. Or, God could be characterized by both kindness and anger. Or, finally, God could be given to anger but not kind. Lactantius feels safe in dismissing this final option. No one had ever advocated such a god, who would only be able to harm and never do good to people, but was simply a torturer and executioner.

Lactantius identifies the first position, the absence in God of both kindness and anger, with the school of Epicurus. Epicurus rightly recognized that kindness and anger go hand in hand, that without anger there can be no kindness, since anyone "who is not subject to anger is plainly uninfluenced by kindness which is the opposite feeling to anger."[54] But unwilling to ascribe the vice of anger to God, he was consistent in ruling out kindness as well. The uncorrupted and untrammeled bliss of God is a function of not caring about anything so as to be troubled. A surviving fragment of Epicurus' *Sentences* claims:

> The blessed and immortal nature knows no trouble (πράγματα) itself nor causes trouble to any other, so that it is never constrained by anger (ὀργή) or favour (χάρις). For all such things exist only in the weak (ἐν ἀσθενεῖ).[55]

A series of rhetorical questions makes Lactantius' estimation of this view of God plain:

> What happiness, then, can there be in God, if He is always inactive, being at rest and unmoveable? If He is deaf to those who pray to Him, and

---

54. Lactantius, *Wrath of God*, p. 4.
55. Epicurus, *Sententiae* 1. *Wrath of God* 8; Paul Gavrilyuk, *The Suffering of the Impassible God: The Dialectics of Patristic Thought* (Oxford: Oxford University Press, 2003), p. 24.

blind to His worshipers? What is so worthy of God, and befitting to Him, as providence? But if He cares for nothing, and foresees nothing, He has lost all divinity.[56]

To do away with anger and kindness is to do away with fear, joy, grief, and pity. Once all affection is removed, God is incapable of caring or ruling providentially.

The Stoics arrive at better sentiments, but lack Epicurus' consistency. They deny God anger, but teach divine kindness and providence. For the Stoic school,

> God is not subject to such littleness of mind as to imagine that He is injured by any one, since it is impossible for Him to be injured; so that the serene and holy majesty is excited, disturbed, and maddened, which is part of human frailty. For they say that anger is a commotion and perturbation of the mind, which is inconsistent with God.[57]

Lactantius recognizes the attractiveness of this sentiment and knows its popularity, but the reasoning is specious. If God has no anger toward the unrighteous, then love for the righteous becomes meaningless. According to Lactantius, "it is necessary to be moved to both sides or to neither." So the Stoics should have concluded, "because God is moved by kindness, therefore He is also liable to anger." The Stoics tear asunder what God has joined together.

> Thus, he who loves the good also hates the evil, and he who does not hate the evil does not love the good, because, on the one hand, to love the good comes from hatred of evil, and to hate the evil rises from love of the good. There is no one who loves life without a hatred of death, and no one seeks light but he flees darkness; for those things are so connected by nature that one cannot exist without the other.[58]

The simplistic reasoning of Lactantius' dialect is likely to sound unpersuasive to our ears. Yet, there is much at stake in the soundness of Lactantius' conclusion. He arrives at the only remaining position: that God

56. Lactantius, *Wrath of God* 4. Lactantius' critique of Epicurus strongly echoes Cicero's in *The Nature of the Gods*, 1.121-22.
57. Lactantius, *Wrath of God* 5 [McDonald].
58. Lactantius, *Wrath of God* 5 [McDonald].

is moved by kindness and anger in his relationship to his creatures. This puts Lactantius out of step with the philosophers, but he is compelled to hold to this conviction because it is so fundamental:

> for upon it rests the sum total, and it is the hinge of piety and religion. And neither can any honour be owed to God if He grants nothing to one worshiping him, nor any fear if He does not become angry with one who does not worship him.[59] (*Wrath of God* 6 [Donaldson])

This conviction carries very significant implications. In his major work, the *Institutes*, he writes:

> Hence the view of some people that God does not even get angry, because he is not subject to emotions, which are disturbances of the mind: all creatures liable to emotional affect are frail. That belief destroys truth and religion utterly.[60]

For Lactantius, "That is how we know we matter to God: he gets angry when we sin."[61]

It becomes vital to recognize that the strength of this conviction does not rely solely on a simplistic process of elimination. When he repeats a similarly sweeping claim in his treatise on God's anger, he adds: "All the prophets, being filled with the Divine Spirit, speak nothing else than the favour of God towards the righteous, and his anger against the ungodly. And their testimony is indeed sufficient for us." However, since the Old Testament prophets would produce no effect on his imagined pagan audience he seeks instead "those testimonies which they can either believe, or at any rate not oppose."[62] So, instead of the Scriptures, Lactantius draws his proof from the Sibylline Oracles, Aristo, Apollodorus, and Varro.

We are left to imagine which Old Testament texts Lactantius had in mind, but a cursory reading of the Scriptures confirms his claim. He may have easily begun with Exodus 34:6-7, the great "read my lips" text:

> The LORD passed before him, and proclaimed,
> "The LORD, the LORD,

59. Lactantius, *Wrath of God* 6 [McDonald].
60. Lactantius, *Inst.* 2.17.2-5 [Bowen and Garnsey].
61. Lactantius, *Inst.* 5.22.13.
62. Lactantius, *Wrath of God* 22.

a God merciful and gracious,
slow to anger,
and abounding in steadfast love and faithfulness,
keeping steadfast love for the thousandth generation,
forgiving iniquity and transgression and sin,
yet by no means clearing the guilty,
but visiting the iniquity of the parents
upon the children and the children's children,
to the third and the fourth generation."

Again and again in the Scriptures, anger and mercy are assumed to be two sides of the one coin.[63] Just in case "slowness to anger" is misunderstood, the chronicler accounts for the great disaster of Israel's history in these terms:

> The LORD, the God of their ancestors, sent persistently to them by his messengers, because he had compassion on his people and on his dwelling place; but they kept mocking the messengers of God, despising his words, and scoffing at his prophets, until the wrath of the LORD against his people became so great that there was no remedy. Therefore he brought up against them the king of the Chaldeans. . . . (2 Chron. 36:15-17)

As Paul warns,

> Or do you despise the riches of his kindness and forbearance and patience? Do you not realize that God's kindness is meant to lead you to repentance? But by your hard and impenitent heart you are storing up wrath for yourself on the day of wrath, when God's righteous judgment will be revealed. (Rom. 2:4-5)

Or consider the words of Jesus:

63. Do not let anything devoted to destruction stick to your hand, so that the LORD may turn from his fierce anger and show you compassion, and in his compassion multiply you, as he swore to your ancestors. (Deut. 13:17)

In overflowing wrath for a moment I hid my face from you, but with everlasting love I will have compassion on you, says the LORD, your Redeemer. (Isa. 54:8)

What if God, desiring to show his wrath and to make known his power, has endured with much patience the objects of wrath that are made for destruction; and what if he has done so in order to make known the riches of his glory for the objects of mercy, which he has prepared beforehand for glory — including us whom he has called, not from the Jews only but also from the Gentiles? (Rom. 9:22-24)

Whoever believes in the Son has eternal life; whoever disobeys the Son will not see life, but must endure God's wrath. (John 3:36)

The Consolations of Theology

For all his purported mediocrity, there is comfort to be found in Lactantius' reflections on the problem of anger. He places the phenomenon squarely within a world created by God and a matrix of relationships intended by him. In doing so he reflects theologically, bringing what the Scriptures say about divine anger to bear. His refusal to cite relevant biblical texts will always render him unfashionable for our discussions, but this should not exempt us from grappling with whether he does reflect God's revelation. Hallman summarizes his contribution thus:

> Lactantius squarely faces the question of divine emotions and mutability. He argues that God must relate to the world in a providential manner, and that this relation must include emotions. Both he and Tertullian saw, however, that God must have emotions only in some distinctively divine manner, either by feeling only the most appropriate emotions or by having all emotions perfectly.[64]

In conclusion, I want to offer six areas of consolation for angry people. They are arranged in three dialectical pairs, in the hope of charting a course that acknowledges the goodness of God's gift and its capacity for harm.

1a. Our Capacity for Anger Is a Good Gift from God

Lactantius reminds us that anger is a good gift from God, an impulse implanted in us at creation. It is part of our faculty for recognizing and resisting sin in our communities and the lives of people under our care. It is not something that God expects us to uproot, but to exercise in our struggle against sin. Sin's corruption of this impulse should not obscure its essential goodness, and its capacity for invigorating and energizing our lives to do God's will.

---

64. Joseph M. Hallman, *The Descent of God: Divine Suffering in History and Theology* (Minneapolis: Fortress, 1991), p. 74.

The very volatility of anger is God's good gift to spur us on to a life of self-control and love. Experiences of anger force us to cultivate our hearts and harness its power for good. Its energizing power does have the potential for enormous harm, rendering each of us potential little Chernobyls. Yet, it is possible to be angry and not sin. In fact, we are commanded to respond angrily in some situations so that offenses and provocations are dealt with quickly.

Furthermore, anger registers our care for people and situations. Our engagement in love with people around us will inevitably bring us into situations where we are wronged, offended, or hurt. It is appropriate that we respond with feelings of offense and anger. Yet, this ought to drive us to conversation, to seek reconciliation and ensure that the devil does not get a foothold. Our anger must be mortal, ephemeral, dealt with promptly, serving as an impulse to remove the sin that disfigures our fellowship with each other and God.

1b. As We Experience Anger, God Is Committed to Conforming Us to the Image of His Son

For many, anger management constitutes one of the great struggles, an ongoing source of shame. Perhaps in the last week you have had some volcanic confrontation that has left you defeated: words spoken to a spouse, a child, or a co-worker. The God who gave the gift of anger, who calls us to be angry but not sin, is committed to your expressing anger in appropriate ways. In his kindness, for instance, through the Psalms, our Father invites us to vent our frustrations and irritations to him. The Spirit who is grieved whenever we give the devil a foothold is committed to reshaping the way we regulate and express anger, so we remain free of the terrible spiral into bitterness, wrangling, slander, and malice.

Perhaps today is the day to acknowledge that this is a problem that needs to be dealt with. Perhaps that means no longer taking refuge in excuses or rationalizations. Very often, my anger confronts me with my pettiness and self-centeredness, realities I would rather not face. Perhaps there are specific relationships that you need to go and address, seeking forgiveness or the opportunity to put away your anger. For some of us, the problem will be deep-seated, originating in dysfunctional family relationships or some kind of mental illness. It may be that you need to seek the kind of professional help that God has provided for people who need this kind of assistance. For all of us it calls for courage; the courage to tune in to our responses, to take responsibility for them, seek help, and address the issues.

The consolation of theology is that God cares deeply and underwrites his good gifts with the good-est gift, the Holy Spirit. God is determined to conform you to the image of his Son, not someone free of anger, but someone able to control anger and express it righteously. Here is great consolation.

2a. In Christian Communities, Anger Ought to Be Directed at Sin

In the midst of numerous warnings of the danger of human anger, we are commanded to be angry in some situations. If Wallace's exegesis of Ephesians 4:26-27 is sound, then these verses constitute a call to resist sin by quickly dealing with offenses.

We, more than any generation before us, are aware of the horrors committed in Christian churches: the sexual abuse of children, teenagers, and vulnerable congregation members; the manipulation of church finances to embezzle huge amounts of money; the authoritarian leadership that bullies congregation members; the complacent abuse of power. It is a list we would rather turn away from than face. And none of us are beyond temptation in these and other areas. Sadly, too often, too little has been done, too late.

It is appropriate that we respond angrily to these things. It is righteous anger that reflects the anger of God that ought to impel us to act, to be vigilant, to listen carefully to those who claim to be victims, to ensure the accused are treated with justice, to act quickly to ensure that sin does not spread like gangrene. Of course, this ought to be mediated and restrained by appropriate legal process.

2b. In Christian Communities, the Word of Christ Protects Us from the Excesses of Anger

Undoubtedly, some will be anxious about the implications of insisting on a place for anger. Perhaps your scars are precisely from the unrestrained and destructive expression of anger by leaders and congregation members who insisted their anger was justified and righteous. Here there is enormous danger, but Lactantius urges readers to resist the attractive solution that we uproot anger altogether.

As together we seek to face the issues raised by anger, our shared lives are governed by the stern words of Jesus and the apostles: "if you are angry with a brother or sister, you will be liable to judgment"; be "slow to speak, slow to anger, for your anger does not produce God's righteousness"; "be angry, but do not sin." We need to be protected from human anger. There is enormous potential for harm. Yet, it will inevitably arise as we genuinely engage and care for one another. It is through the riches of the gospel and the consolations of theology that God equips us to use it for good and not evil.

There is no future in denial and repression. In our congregations, lives and families are being torn apart by the inability of people, even believers, to understand and express their anger. In the Holy Spirit, the Scriptures, and our fellowship together we have the resources to grapple with anger.

3a. We Live in a World Ruled by a God Who Is Angry at Sin and Evil

Lactantius' philosophical heritage was ill-equipped to fashion a god who cared profoundly for the world. In the Scriptures we find a God who dignifies our lives by caring enough to be angry at our rebellion and destructive choices, yet meets our desperate need with kindness and compassion. God will not allow evil to triumph, a reality Lactantius detected in the downfall of persecuting emperors. While we rightly hesitate to read God's will from the pages of history, Lactantius points to the sovereign providence of God over all human history, his vindication of his oppressed people, and his angry prosecution of evil.

There is rich consolation in observing Jesus' angry unmasking of religious hypocrisy and cant (Mark 3:5); his indignant admonition of his disciples when they engage in the same politics of exclusion (Mark 10:14); his seething outside the tomb of his dear friend Lazarus (John 11:33). He is amply worthy of our worship; and in his anger at corruption, sin, and death, he is our champion.

We can rest in God's wrath (Rom. 12:19). Vengeance is God's, not ours.

This is a liberating message for those who live in a world where the cycles of vengeance threaten to destroy the fabric of our families, our societies, and the world. We can leave vengeance to the one who sees all and judges every situation justly. God will not leave the guilty unpunished and will vindicate the righteous. We can rest on the fact that God will pursue wrongdoers angrily, until they face the consequences of their selfishness.

3b. In the Death of His Son, God's Righteous Anger Was Propitiated

How can we rest in God's wrath when Jesus warns us that our failure to control our anger renders us liable to judgment? What hope is there for people prone to exercising God's good gift in selfish and abusive ways? Theology's ultimate consolation comes to us at the cross, where God's anger and mercy meet to make life available to people who deserve judgment. Jesus' death was a propitiatory sacrifice, turning God's anger away from us.

Whether it is due to his mediocrity or his literary strategy, it is a pity that Lactantius does not make more of this great truth. Jesus is unambiguously the Savior in his writings, and forgiveness the great need of sinners. However, he tends to emphasize earnest reformation of life by the individual, rather than the atoning death of Jesus, as the grounds for God's mercy. No doubt this is, to some extent, a function of his audience and strategy. But his discussion of divine and human anger would be greatly enhanced by anchoring it in the cross of Christ, "whom God put forward as a sacrifice of atonement by his blood, effective through faith" (Rom. 3:25).

The cross is the appropriate terminus for this discussion of how we deal with anger. The most difficult experiences of anger we face are those where we cannot shake the conviction that we are justified in feeling angry and the prospect of revenge seems right and sweet. It is the cross that allows us, no, demands of us, that we put down our weapons and let go of our anger. There God's righteous anger against us was appeased. Now he calls us to the same forgiveness, so that our relationships are ruled by grace and kindness rather than bitterness and revenge.

For we worship the God who is slow to anger, and rich in mercy, the Father of compassion and the God of all consolation.

AUGUSTINE
on Obsession

ANDREW CAMERON

Beloved, I urge you as aliens and exiles to abstain from the desires of the flesh that wage war against the soul.

1 Peter 2:11

1. A Portrait of Obsession

In the 1998 movie *A Simple Plan*, midwestern U.S. couple Hank and Sarah try to control events after Hank's discovery of a downed plane buried in a snow-covered forest, and the duffel bag within it full of four million dollars in hundred-dollar notes. It turns out that what can least be controlled is their own response. Hank's ominous opening soliloquy signals their descent:

> When I was still just a kid, I remember my father telling me what he thought that it took for a man to be happy. Simple things, really. A wife he loves; a decent job; friends and neighbors who like and respect him. For a while there, without hardly even realizing it, I had all that. I was a happy man.

But as much as being about Hank, the movie charts his wife Sarah's journey, and her loss of that simple happiness. Actress Bridget Fonda describes the way a stranger's money causes Sarah to spiral out of control:

1. *A Simple Plan*, Mutual Film Company/Paramount 1998; DVD imprint, Magna Pacific/Becker Entertainment.

She's basically put her wish list on hold, and was very happy, and things were good. They're going to have a baby, they're going to have a life together and she *loves* her husband, and it doesn't get any better than that — until you're faced with the possibility that it *might* get better than that. And then once you embrace that . . . it creeps in, and you can't help it — your mind starts to get *mesmerized* by the idea of it, and before you know it, it's yours, and in your head you've already spent it, and so then what do you do? You do anything to hang onto it, because to have it — something that's not even yours to begin with — to have it taken away is like having part of yourself cut out, because already in your mind you've spent it on your child's education, on a vacation, on a better house with a bigger yard, and you have these dreams for this little baby. . . .[2]

In *A Simple Plan*, Hank and Sarah are, in the first instance, exemplars of greed. But as Fonda depicts this greed, it is mesmeric, invasive, and ingrown. Its fantasy visions become indivisible from the self — vital, it seems, for life to continue. Sarah is in the vortex of something more than just greed, and her experience points beyond greed to the experience we'll be calling *obsession*.

An older encyclopedist, James Hastings, sums up the sudden and disturbing and very arbitrary nature of our obsessions when he says that:

An obsession is a dissociated idea, or group of ideas, which suddenly enters consciousness, disturbing the ordinary course of ideation, but not involving the personality of the individual — that is to say, the subject of the obsession regards it as an unreality, and as apart from his ordinary ideation. . . . The number of obsessions is endless, there being almost as many forms as there are of thought. Some are harmless and meaningless, as, *e.g.*, the desire to repeat certain words or phrases, to count objects of no interest, or to touch certain articles. Others are fateful, as the desire to kill, to commit suicide, or to steal.[3]

But his definition of *obsession* appears under his entry for "insanity." A modern psychologist might find several reasons to quibble, because Hastings mentions what today would be called "obsessive-compulsive dis-

2. DVD feature interview.
3. James Hastings, ed., *Encyclopaedia of Religion and Ethics*, vol. 7 (Hymns-Liberty) (Edinburgh: T. & T. Clark, 1914), p. 243.

order" (OCD), and perhaps some psychotic disorders. However, Hastings is correct to highlight the great number of obsessions available to us, and alongside the kleptomania and the repetitive obsessions, we could easily and recognizably include Sarah's obsession with a better life built on money that isn't hers.

Hastings could also have listed a character in P. G. Wodehouse, Corky's uncle, who owned a business dealing in jute (a kind of vegetable fiber from which hessian or burlap is made):

> Corky's uncle, you see, didn't want him to be an artist. He didn't think he had any talent in that direction. He was always urging him to chuck Art and go into the jute business and start at the bottom and work his way up. Jute had apparently become a sort of obsession with him. He seemed to attach almost a spiritual importance to it. *(My Man Jeeves)*

We could list billionaire Howard Hughes, whose legendary obsession with hygiene extended to scrubbing telephones and preventing others from touching the knobs on his television. Basketball player Michael Jordan has been described as "one of the most competitive human beings ever seen," turning anything that can be competitive into a competition that he must win.[4] Perhaps Shirley MacLaine's description of her five-year-old rat terrier as her "soul mate" might be listed among the obsessions. Her soul mate is also, we are assured, the coauthor of her biography. MacLaine first met the dog in Egypt in a past life, when she was a "minor princess" and the dog was a canine god. (We know this because the dog wrote that part of the book.)[5]

An older man's obsession with his vintage cars; a youth's obsession with his computer game; a young girl's obsession to be listed among a small knot of friends; a middle-aged man's obsession with his secretary; a sports fan's obsession with a grand final win. Even something as innocent as sunbathing can, we are told, become an obsession. So-called "tanorexics" have been identified, who display addictive tendencies similar to alcoholics or compulsive gamblers, with one dermatologist seeing patients who have had melanomas cut out but still cannot quit. "They're out of

---

4. BBC World Service, "Beyond Sport (Part 1)," *Documentary Archive:* 2006, 12' 30".

5. [Author unnamed], "Terms of Enjoyment," *Reader's Digest* October 2005; online: http://www.rd.com/content/openContent.do?contentId=28679&pageIndex=0 (accessed 19/9/2006).

control, and they're not just being naughty; they've got a problem and they need professional help."[6]

The objectives of these obsessions might span the moral spectrum from innocent to deeply worrying, but they are all at the extreme end of the intensity spectrum. These are whole-body desires that wage war against our very selves.

Usage of the English term "obsession" can be found five centuries ago, as when those in a castle sent word to advise that they were "obsessed," which is to say *under siege,* by an enemy. The word eventually became a description of what evil spirits do: just as enemies obsess castles, evil spirits "obsess" people, laying siege to them and enticing them to act in various compulsive ways. Since then the word has come to describe a mind plagued by a fixed idea or an unwanted or unhelpful desire. It refers to those episodes in life where we were deep in the grip of some "passion" that we often look back upon with a rueful shake of our heads and say, "I don't know what I was thinking of." We were "under siege."

The biblical languages have no direct equivalent for the term "obsession," and translators only reach for it occasionally. Paul's "raging fury" (ἐμμαίνομαι, Acts 26:11); or the false teacher's "morbid craving" for controversy (νοσέω, 1 Tim. 6:4); or the weak woman's being "weighed down" with sins (σωρεύω, 2 Tim. 3:6) are each called "obsessions" in various different translations.[7]

But before any consideration can be made of the texture of biblical "obsession," we must ask whether it is simply mistaken to group so many experiences together under this concept of "obsession." People like to think that "anger" is a little more circumscribed, and that it is relatively straightforward whether we or others are angry (although Lactantius teaches us that our anger probably isn't as straightforward as we like to imagine). But as a category, "obsession" is more problematic. Long ago, astronomers used the mistaken category of "superlunary objects," or those that were outside the orbit of the moon. But the category was not just too broad to be of any use — it failed as a term of description because "objects outside the orbit of the moon" is not a class with any seri-

6. Dr. Tony White, senior lecturer in the Department of Dermatology at Sydney University, interviewed by Amy Lawson, "Sun Addicts Need AA-Type Program," *The Sunday Age* 2 October 2005, p. 5.

7. Respectively, New International Version, New King James Version, and New Jerusalem Bible.

ous or useful reality to it.[8] Do we risk the same problem with the term "obsession"?

I have chosen to keep "obsession" under scrutiny, because when we try to discard it we find that there remain these *interests and attachments, whether good or bad, that somehow "get beyond us," where we are then out of control.* That phenomenon, like anything else in the world, is worth subjecting to the analysis of Christian thought; but more pressingly, the phenomenon is painful and pervasive, and desperately invites the consolations of theology. **What makes us obsess like this, and how can we stop?**

2. Absolutizing the Dark Side of Desire

It would be hard work to map the semantic connections between the NT Greek and modern English for strong, obsessional desire. One useful way forward is to examine the Bible's use of the term ἐπιθυμία (generally glossed as "passion," or "desire"). Of course there are more terms for "strong desire" than this, with one team of lexicographers finding over twenty words inhabiting the conceptual field of "strong desire." But to examine just ἐπιθυμία is to act like an archaeologist, who sinks a narrow shaft deep into a broad dig-site. We could later go on to dig elsewhere, but in this important shaft we will find major biblical texts that help us to understand desire, and in turn, obsession.

We will also find misreadings of these texts that have produced a distorted and sub-Christian account of desire. I call this distortion the "absolutizing of the dark side of desire." We may catch a glimpse of the distorted account if we glance at 1 Peter 2:11 and ask, is *every* desire that bubbles up from your human flesh opposed to your soul? Whoever answers "yes" has made the dark side of human desire become an absolute description of all human desire.

It is not hard to see why readers of the Bible have made this mistake. Humanity has its perennially favorite desires, ἐπιθυμίαι, such as for money, sex, food, or power. The NT epistles in particular have a bit to say about these, and as a result, NT desire is often guilty by association through col-

---

8. I owe this observation, made in another context (of the term "emotion"), to Paul E. Griffiths, *What Emotions Really Are: The Problem of Psychological Categories* (Chicago: University of Chicago Press, 1997), pp. 14-17 & passim.

location with some negative adjective or verb. It is a word that attracts several negative qualifiers: "deceitful," "lustful," "worldly," "corrupt," "debauched," "ungodly." Desire's work in the human body is portrayed as misleading us, tempting us, enslaving and opposing us. It is devilish, deranged, and self-focused, and puts us under judgment. Such a high volume of negative references, and the fact that it often appears in conversations about human flesh, often leads to the conclusion that the human body and its desires are both straightforwardly evil.

Such a conclusion often made strong headway in the ancient Hellenistic world. In this milieu, desires of flesh waging war against the soul could be understood as an evil body attacking, oppressing, and restraining a good and pure spirit. Not all ancient perceptions of the body and its desires were as bleak as that; nevertheless, Margaret Miles can find a desert father who declares of his own body, "I am killing it because it is killing me."[9]

By the time of the third century, the respectable Christian sect called Manicheism was able to gather people around such bleak views of the body. Manichees were dualists who thought that everything originated from "two masses of good and evil."[10] These two masses are infinite, "the evil in a lesser and the good in a greater degree."[11] We may take a little comfort that the good material outweighs the bad; but not much comfort, because the conflict between the evil substance and the good substance rages within each person, to the point that souls could themselves become materially and substantially corrupted[12] until we escape our bodies.

The Manichees "absolutized" the dark side of desire. Bodily desire is corrupt, because the body itself is corrupt. It is an account that would have explained obsession very straightforwardly: obsession is simply an inevitable result of being in a body, and the only way to escape it is for our spirits to escape our bodies. But although the Manichees could offer this explanation of sorts for desire and obsession, there is no *consolation* at all to be found here.

---

9. Margaret R. Miles, *Augustine on the Body*, vol. 31 (Missoula: Scholars Press, 1979), p. 131, citing Heraclides, *Paradeisos* I.

10. Augustine, *Confessions*, trans. R. S. Pine-Coffin, *Penguin Classics* edition (Harmondsworth: Penguin, 1961), p. 106 (V.11).

11. Augustine, *Confessions*, p. 104 (V.10).

12. Augustine, *Confessions*, p. 135 (VII.2).

Excursus
A Brief Biography of Augustine

The man we may thank for driving this sub-Christian view of ourselves from the field is Augustine, Bishop of Hippo in North Africa during the late fourth and early fifth centuries.[13] He has been described as "far and away the best — if not the very first — psychologist in the ancient world."[14] (If theologians judge "psychology" as untheological, and unworthy of the attention of some, warrant for their judgments can only be found in the twentieth century. "Soul science" had a long and distinguished theological history prior to that.[15])

There is so much to identify with in Augustine. In his *Confessions* we meet him as a lower middle-class boy growing up on the edge of the civilized world. His pagan father, Patricius, wants him educated for success, with his emotionally intense mother, Monica, wanting him to follow Jesus and to marry a nice Christian girl. In a story that many young adults will still relate to, he travels far from home and abandons all self-control during his "college" years. He fathers a son to his live-in-lover, then breaks up with her for another — his mother badgering him all the while to follow Jesus and to marry a nice Christian girl. Meanwhile Augustine sharpens his rhetoric, searches for truth, stays up late with friends, and gets lost in careerism. But then he hears a preacher, Ambrose of Milan, who has the truth for which he yearns; and in a rapidly escalating series of events, Monica's prayers are answered, and Augustine turns to Christ.

He was a thinker, a writer, and a reader, and his first impulse was to start something like the L'Abri fellowship with a few friends, in a country

13. For a helpful summary of Augustine's biography (taken mainly from the *Confessions*), see the blog by Michael A. G. Haykin, *Eminent Christians: 12. Augustine of Hippo* (online: http://mghhistor.blogspot.com/2006/09/eminent-christians-augustine-of-hippo.html, accessed 19/09/2006). The definitive biography is Peter Brown, *Augustine of Hippo: A Biography (A New Edition with an Epilogue)* (London: Faber, 2000).

14. Albert C. Outler, ed., *Augustine: Confessions and Enchiridion*, vol. 7, Library of Christian Classics (London: SCM Press, 1955), p. 15; online: http://www.fordham.edu/halsall/basis/confessions-bod.html (accessed 13/5/2006).

15. For a fascinating account of the way a thick "Christian psychology" was supplanted by thin secularist versions (such as behaviorism), see Thomas Dixon, "Theology, Anti-Theology and Atheology: From Christian Passions to Secular Emotions," *Modern Theology* 15, no. 3 (1999).

villa not far from the northern Italian Alps, near the town of Cassiciacum. Yet this cozy plan is soon overtaken by events, and within a few years he finds himself pressed into service first as priest, then as bishop, to the slightly desperate little church of Hippo Regius on the North African coast. After all the cosmopolitan glamour of his travels, he finds himself in this little ministry only about two hundred kilometers from his hometown.

Although he began his life in the stately Indian summer of the old Roman Empire, he straddles the fault line of his age, the September 11 of the ancient world: the sack of Rome in AD 410. The attackers do not really do much damage, and really only want some ransom money; but the psychological effect is devastating, for Rome is supposedly "the eternal city" that has stretched back over a thousand years. In response Augustine begins to write the *City of God,* a multivolume epic that contrasts Rome's passing shabbiness to the truly eternal city of God, to which God is shepherding his people — and any Romans who want to come, too. The book consolidates his role as one of Christianity's most gleeful apologists.

But his workday life in ministry sees obsession from all angles. Augustine's ongoing attempts to curb the voracity of one Antoninus, the young bishop of Fussala on the rural outskirts of Hippo, highlights Augustine's integrity and care in response to damage caused by the obsession of another. In Peter Brown's summary,

> The upshot of repeated attempts to investigate and discipline Antoninus was that, in the hot late summer of 422, Augustine found himself stranded for weeks on end in the middle of a countryside where everyone spoke only Punic. He visited the village of Fussala, where the inhabitants pointed out to him the holes in the houses from which Antoninus had pillaged the stones in order to build a splendid new episcopal palace. He was finally left, sitting alone one morning in a village church after the entire congregation had walked out in disgust — even . . . the nuns — leaving him and his colleagues to wonder how, by what series of misjudgments exploited by an able rogue, they had brought "so much sadness upon the country people."[16]

Augustine was also involved in ongoing attempts to stop the illegal enslavement of North African Romans, in a quest for justice that sought even to protect the slavers, who also bore God's image, from being summarily

16. Brown, *Augustine* (new ed.), p. 469, citing Augustine's letter.

executed.[17] These vignettes, when placed alongside his extant sermons numbering in the hundreds, show that the Augustine who matters most to us was not the pretentious young philosopher of Cassiciacum, but a daily-grind pastor and preacher.

The theological battles he fights derive from the same kind of love for neighbor that had sent him to Fussala. Straight after his conversion, he can no longer abide the bleak folly and stupidity of the Manichees, who simply ignore God's declaration of Genesis 1:31, that the human body is *good*.

A long time after that and quite late in his life we find the same love for his neighbor driving Augustine into battle against the sternly moral Pelagians, who claim that God would not command what we cannot do, and that a man armed with God's word in the Bible, and with the power of an obedient will, possesses all that is needed to please God. By this stage, Augustine has seen enough obsessions to know that the body may be good, but it is also *unremittingly fallen*, and that any attempt to imagine a morally self-sufficient Christian is simply to claim that Christ died for no good reason. Pelagian optimism must be making the claim that "Christ died in vain" (Gal. 2:21).

His pastoral engagements are therefore played out against a sweeping backdrop of high-stakes battle against two deeply different anthropological malfunctions, seen first in the bleak Manichees and then in the smug Pelagians. It is this "story arc" to Augustine's life that forges one of the first and very best psychologists, who is in a good position to deliver theology's true consolation to obsession.

3. Augustine's Account of Obsession

Augustine spends a lot of time explaining desire.[18] We have proper longings for God the Father, for each other, and for all the goods of a good earth. But these proper longings are distorted and disordered into improper longings, many of which we call "obsessions." But the good news is that even with disordered desires, we can yet be redeemed by Christ, and then gently reordered by the power of the Spirit.

17. Brown, *Augustine*, pp. 466, 470-71.
18. I am grateful to my former doctoral supervisor, the Revd. Dr. Michael Banner, for his many insights into Augustine's account of obsession.

What the NT called ἐπιθυμία, Augustine called "concupiscence" (Latin *libido*). Theological history has seen the term "concupiscence" harden into a rather impersonal and technical term. But it did not begin there for Augustine.

He noticed the way an infant is "pale with envy" at his sibling on the breast. The infant "object[s] to a rival's finding life in this nourishment, even when the milk flows in such abundance from its source."[19] Everyone objects at this point, with the Pelagians, that we shouldn't bring babies into it or that this behavior is a natural drive. But those objections seriously miss the point. Augustine tolerates such behaviors and knows that children will grow out of them. But it will grow *into* other powerful desires, and he can detect no turning point or dividing line when people cross from some innocent natural contentment into some corrupted adult concupiscence. Rather, the essence of concupiscence colors every human from the day of their birth, and all their relationships every day thereafter.

It surprises many to discover that sexual desire was *not* Augustine's paradigm case for concupiscence. Indeed, he does not find it surprising or even particularly interesting that people like sex (and in his overall corpus, discussions of sex are scattered and often short). Rather, the case that truly mystifies him is the episode from his childhood when he and his friends stole a farmer's pears:

> [O]f what I stole I already had plenty, and much better at that, and I had no wish to enjoy [them.] . . . We took away an enormous quantity of pears, not to eat them ourselves, but simply to throw them to the pigs.[20]

> This was friendship of a most unfriendly sort, bewitching my mind in an inexplicable way. For the sake of a laugh, a little sport, I was glad to do harm and anxious to damage another; and that without thought of profit for myself or retaliation for injuries received! And all because we are ashamed to hold back when others say "Come on! Let's do it!"[21]

Detractors may again sigh, "Oh Augustine — you were only boys." But again, the objector misses the point: this boy's extreme longing to belong has distorted his capacity to evaluate what is before him, such as the dam-

19. Augustine, *Conf.*, p. 28 (I.7).
20. Augustine, *Conf.*, p. 47 (II.4).
21. Augustine, *Conf.*, p. 52 (II.9).

age to the farmer. This wearisome aspect of human life, where entrancement with some passing good blinds us to something greater, plagues us from the momentary obsessions of our childhood to the very destructive obsessions of adulthood.

We are each situated within an ordered ecology of interdependent goods, and humans are the kind of beings who respond to those goods with the various desires, interests, cares, concerns, and attractions that Augustine is content simply to call "love." Various "aspects" of love can be identified (since the term covers many kinds of response to the plethora of goods that surround people); and people's basic propensity to respond in love to the goods of creation is central to being human.

Indeed, Augustine thinks it is obvious that each person incarnates an inalienable, irreducible, and essential impulse to love. Our capacities to exist, to know, and to love are the most properly basic attributes of humanity;[22] but whereas philosophy then as now concentrates upon the first two of these attributes, Augustine thinks that attention to the third has been neglected. Humanity's deep care about right and wrong, as well as people's insistence upon various acts, both signal the fundamental human capacity to love.

But these various possibilities for love also form the seeds of obsession at the core of our soul. One of Augustine's reflections on ἐπιθυμία begins quite obliquely, and looks at first like an early treatise on perception.[23] He marvels at the way his senses could gather sights and sounds and store them in the "vast cave" of his memory. Even one so beautiful as God could make his home there, in his mind. Yet this "fleshly" system, although wonderfully good, is also riddled with possibilities for subversion.

- Firstly, *our senses* can become trapped in what they sense. Many of us will recognize this lifelong task of Augustine's: "I struggle daily against greed for food and drink." "I must therefore hold back my appetite with neither too firm nor too slack a rein."[24] Likewise fragrances, music, and sensual sensations all have their place; yet he was not happy about the way all of these could claim and mesmerize him.
- Secondly, he thinks *scientific inquisitiveness* can go too far. He becomes

22. Augustine, *The City of God Against the Pagans*, trans. R. W. Dyson, *Cambridge Texts in the History of Political Thought* edition (Cambridge: Cambridge University Press, 1998), p. 488 (XI.28).

23. Augustine, *Conf.*, Book X.

24. Augustine, *Conf.*, p. 237 (X.31).

unduly engrossed in the sight of a dog chasing a hare, or of a lizard eating a fly. Modern readers may think Augustine is silly to chide himself for such interests, and even he knows that they can result in proper praise to God for the creation.[25] But he senses a weakness here: that such a distraction can become a fixation, then an obsession.

• Because we are like this, "there is a third kind of temptation which, I fear, has not passed from me. Can it ever pass from me in all this life? It is the desire to be feared or loved by other men, simply for the pleasure that it gives me, though in such pleasure there is no true joy."[26] Like many of us, he is easily ensnared into *social obsessions,* and his autobiography is loaded with examples. "I was preparing a speech in praise of the Emperor, intending that it should include a great many lies which would certainly be applauded by an audience who knew well enough how far from the truth they were." "My ambitions had placed a load of misery on my shoulders and the further I carried it the heavier it became" — and then, to his shock, he passes a drunken beggar who is freer and happier than he.[27]

Obsessions begin with substances and experiences, with knowledge and its acquisition, and with social acceptance and social power. The problem is not that these are bad; on the contrary, according to Genesis 1:31, God made everything "very good" in its own place. But everything is almost *too* good; and we are surrounded by it, and so have all been, or are, obsessed by some aspect of this abundant goodness.

Augustine suggests that if we are honest with ourselves, there is a seamlessness between the kind of momentary "obsessions" that lure him throughout the day — the food, the lizard, the praise of other men — and the obsessions that ended up enslaving us (of which in his case, sex is an example). If we allow Augustine's way of thinking to guide us, we begin to see how innocent enthusiasms can segue, for example, into relentless careerism and then appalling destruction. Instead then of mocking Augustine for being over-rigorous about his fascination in the lizard, we might notice the way another generation of scientists' initial fascination with the atom gave way to industrious experimentation and theory formation upon it, and finally to its

25. Augustine, *Conf.,* p. 243 (X.35).
26. Augustine, *Conf.,* p. 244 (X.36).
27. Augustine, *Conf.,* p. 118 (VI.6).

destructive uses in atomic warfare that many scientists went on to condemn. The same story repeats itself today, as when an interest in the human embryo and an intention to heal men and women in the pain of infertility becomes the generation of tens of thousands of extra embryos, and then a justification for destructive research upon them, cloning of them, and the mating of non-human animal material with them. An initial and very proper fascination seamlessly drifts into what has clearly become a form of obsession for dozens of scientists around the world — an obsession, we might surmise, that is not untouched by "the desire to be feared or loved by" other scientists and politicians, "simply for the pleasure that it gives."

It turns out that Augustine has been doing a threefold analysis of obsession based upon John's threefold description of our human response to the world (1 John 2:16):

the desires of the flesh and the desires of the eyes and pride in possessions

— or, as a more racy translation puts it,

a craving for physical pleasure, a craving for everything we see, and pride in our achievements and possessions.

These powerful cravings are what theology calls *concupiscence:* those strong and overwhelming mixtures of mental and emotional longing that waylay us. (Augustine says that the craving for *money,* as seen in *A Simple Plan,* is explained by the way it enables us to buy into each of these three first cravings.) Augustine can therefore make this powerful mature statement, which occurs just after he mentions sexual lust (the *first* mention of it, we should note, fourteen whole books into the *City of God*). In this quotation, the word "lust" is exactly the same as the word "concupiscence" *(libido):*

[L]ust is the general name for desire of every kind. . . . [T]here is the lust for vengeance, called anger. Again, there is the lust for money, called avarice; the lust for victory at any price, called obstinacy; the lust for glory, called vanity. There are many different kinds of lust, of which not a few have names peculiar to themselves, while others have not. Who, for example, could easily give a name to the lust for mastery, though the evidence of civil wars shows how great a sway it has over the minds of tyrants?[28]

28. Augustine, *City of God,* pp. 613-14 (XIV.15, final paragraph).

His reference to tyrants and their "lust for mastery" *(libido dominandi)* signals the weight of his objection to Rome, its greatness, and its violence-riddled *Pax Romana:* all of these are concupiscent boys stealing and flinging pears, only writ large. Sexual obsession, while important, is a relatively minor player in this overall story of obsession. Augustine's point is like that of the encyclopedist Hastings: that if we are to live well, we must begin by noticing the vast breadth of good things that we become obsessed about.

Knowing this Augustinian account of desire, we may therefore note with interest the New Jerusalem Bible translation of 1 Peter 2:11, "to keep yourselves free from the disordered natural inclinations that attack the soul."

4. What Obsession Really Blinds Us To

To be in the grip of an obsession is to feel energized, intense, and alive. Whether we are on a sexual conquest, hunting for bargains, or seeking revenge, we are as focused as a hawk upon its prey. For the philosopher Charles Taylor,

> This perversity can be described as a drive to make ourselves the centre of our world, to relate everything to ourselves, to dominate and possess the things which surround us. This is both cause and consequence of a kind of slavery, a condition in which we are in turn dominated, captured by our own obsessions and fascination with the sensible.[29]

The obsessed person's sight bores into some tiny corner of God's good world at the expense of all else (and so another term for it seems to be "idolatry," Col. 3:5). In a world abundantly given to be received with thanks (cf. 1 Tim. 4:4-5), the obsessed acts as if the object of their attention is all there is, and as if there can never be enough of it. Augustine noticed this irony: the infant objects to a rival finding life in the nourishment of his mother's breast, even when the milk flows in such abundance from that place. Obsession blinds us to abundance, and leaves us thinking that the object of our obsession is scarce.

Anne Manne writes with incredulity of a woman who moans "I have to work." But, writes Manne, "I looked about me. We were sitting in an

---

29. Charles Taylor, *Sources of the Self: The Making of the Modern Identity* (Cambridge: Cambridge University Press, 1989), pp. 138-39.

air-conditioned 300-square-metre, multi-bedroom ranch house with several bathrooms. Among the vehicles in the multi-car garage was a 4WD worth $50,000." The house was huge, like much of modern suburbia. "The Great Australian Dream had been transformed into an empty crypt of consumption."[30]

The connections between obsession and the myth of scarcity in God's abundant world are beyond our scope, but to pursue them would first reveal the extent to which so many supposed problems are leveraged on the myth and fear of scarcity, and then the new solutions that become apparent when we discover that our real "problem" is the abundance of what is good.

5. Toward a Quiet Life: "Obsession" Body and Soul

We must return to find theology's consolation to obsession. Is there hope for us? How can we stop?

We saw the way ἐπιθυμία seems so negatively regarded in the Bible. But looking more closely, we find several moments where desire is morally unobjectionable, and indeed in the LXX ἐπιθυμία is used across the moral spectrum, more often positively than negatively. God exhorts his people to eat all the meat they want. Solomon builds whatever he wants. God meets the desires of the king and his people. Even the man whose "quiver is full" can be translated as "having fulfilled desires." The wicked have their boastful cravings, but the righteous, the poor, and the afflicted all have their proper longings too. In the Proverbs, everyone craves — sluggards and young men, the wicked and the righteous — although all crave for different objects; and "desire fulfilled," or "a good desire" according to the LXX, is considered a "tree of life" (13:12).

We also see several NT appearances of strong desire as a form of moral excellence. Disciples, prophets, and angels long to see divine truth; apostles long to see Christ, or to see their people, or for their people to progress in faith; young men rightly long to care for God's people.

Also, a most surprising twist becomes apparent. In the Septuagint's translation of Numbers 11:4 we find ἐπιθυμία used twice in a double-

---

30. Anne Manne, "Sell Your Soul and Spend, Spend, Spend: The Cost of Living in a Material World," *SMH* 14 April 2003.

barreled phrase, an emphatic conjoining of the noun and cognate verb, to describe the strong craving for meat in the desert that resulted in an infamous episode in Israel's history, one of its most spectacular passion-related failures, at a site marked and labeled thereafter as the "The Tombs of Craving." This event is remembered throughout both Testaments in the language of ἐπιθυμία, and becomes the archetypal example of human desire expressed in contempt of God.

But in what may be the entirely unanticipated punch line to this story, Jesus uses ἐπιθυμία in almost the same double-barreled phrase to tell of how ardently he longs to eat the Passover with his disciples (Luke 22:25). Not only can desires be very good; somehow, in Jesus we see the eclipse of obsessive and shortsighted craving with a righteous craving that is every bit as intense.

We are forced to ask: Can such a righteous craving be ours? Can we be free, like him, to crave well? Our own existential conundrum is that since these are our *desires* at work, the very machinery used for self-evaluation and then change is hopelessly compromised. Augustine can only find consolation in God: "Can anything restore me to hope except your mercy?"[31] What is theology's consolation for obsession?

a) *In Christ*

It is easy to be reminded of a certain madman who lived among some tombs. "Night and day among the tombs and in the hills he would cry out and cut himself with stones" (Mark 5:5). At first glance, he is not relevant to our enquiry. His was a special case: a legion of spirits possessed him. This was a special event: Jesus' victory was a sign for that time and place in salvation history. The evil spirits "obsessed" him, to be sure; but is that sufficient reason to keep thinking of him?

In one of theology's most magnificent passages, Augustine points to the advent of a Mediator, someone human enough to know our craving way of death, but godlike enough to walk rightly and to desire well.[32] The work of Jesus upon this legion-possessed man prefigures his work upon other men and women in the gospel. We think the man is unlike us, be-

---

31. Augustine, *Conf.*, p. 244 (X.36).
32. Augustine, *Conf.*, p. 251 (X.43).

cause he cuts himself under the power of another, whereas our obsessions, we like to think, are somehow under *our* control — or, if we are Pelagians, they "should be." But precisely here the gospel declares and reveals the opposite to us: we are obsessed, besieged, by a power greater than us, that in the Bible is personified as "sin." All of our more obvious human obsessions are simply extensions of our incapacity to bring order to our emotions, our thoughts, and our will — or as the Bible would denote the intersection of these three, to our *heart*.

Yet just as in the gospel, it seems that Jesus has actually sought out this man, crossing the lake to hear his shrieking, alien cries, and to make him whole. Jesus Christ is the Mediator who knows how to die for the "powerless," for the "ungodly," at the "right time" (Rom. 5:6), the time they need it most. Jesus Christ is the Mediator who knows how "to save completely those who come to God through him, because he always lives to intercede for them" (Heb. 7:25). The power of Jesus Christ is made clearest in human weakness, when he says, "My grace is sufficient for you" (2 Cor. 12:9). Jesus recreates a legion-obsessed man into a new creation, just as "if anyone is in Christ, he is a new creation; the old has gone, the new has come!" (2 Cor. 5:17).

In the well-known and slightly mawkish fridge magnet, a photograph of footprints on an evening beach is overlaid with the questions of a traveler to his or her traveling companion, "Why was there sometimes only one set of footprints? Where did you go, Lord?" A slightly surprised Jesus responds, "They were *my* footprints, because I was carrying you." This is the first and greatest consolation for obsession that theology has for us: that even at our worst, our most inhuman, and our most deranged, when we are least like him but most need him, he will "carry" each of us. He will "carry" us in the sense of not holding our obsessional sin against us, even then enabling for us real friendship with himself and his Father.

Therefore there is perhaps only one thing sadder than an unbelieving world full of those who cry out and "cut themselves," living out their various obsessions, but without running toward Jesus as did the legion-possessed man. It is the evangelical Christian who gladly tells others of this gospel, yet cannot believe it is for him when he is trapped yet again in front of the blue light of Internet porn; or for her when she obsesses yet again about the thinness of some other woman's body; or for him when he rants inwardly at the adulation and success of his clergy peer; or for her when she longs desperately for the love of a man; or for him when he frets constantly over his ominous growing illness; or for her when the interminable wait for the phone to ring or the grandchildren to visit seems so bitterly and endlessly lonely.

Jesus Christ dies for us, prays for us, is graceful toward us, and is even re-creating us, at our most powerless, ungodly, obsessive, weak, and disordered worst. His gospel is not for those who speak it best, but for those who need it most. "Rightly do I place in him," says Augustine, "my firm hope that you will cure all my ills, through him who sits at your right hand and pleads for us; otherwise I should despair. For my ills are many and great . . . but your medicine is greater indeed."[33] In Christ we are permitted the almost unbelievable expectation that soon, perhaps very soon, we, too, may also sit quietly, like the man obsessed by devils no more, "clothed and in his right mind" (Mark 5:15).

b) Love "Poured In"

To be in Christ opens the way for the Spirit to be poured out in our aid. Augustine was fascinated by the way the working Spirit radically reorients our affections.

> [W]e are assisted by divine aid towards the achievement of righteousness, — not merely because God has given us a law full of good and holy precepts, but because our very will, without which we cannot do any good thing, is assisted and elevated by the importation of the Spirit of grace. . . .[34]

> [By the Spirit] there is formed in [a person's] mind a **delight** in, and a love of, that supreme and unchangeable good which is God, even now while he is still "walking by faith" and not yet "by sight"; in order that . . . he may conceive an **ardent desire** to cleave to his Maker, and may **burn** to enter upon the participation in that true light, that it may go well with him from Him to whom he owes his existence.[35]

---

33. Augustine, *Conf.*, p. 251 (X.43).

34. Augustine, *On the Spirit and the Letter* ed. Philip Schaff, trans. Peter Holmes and Robert E. Wallis, NPNF 1, vol. 5 (Grand Rapids: Eerdmans, 1987; originally published New York, 1887), p. 91 (§20).

35. Augustine, *On the Spirit and the Letter*, p. 84 (§5), emphasis added.

Here is the language of a new "obsession": an "ardent desire" not unlike Jesus at that Passover, and a "burning" to participate in intimate relationship with the same maker as wishes it to go well with us.

Augustine looked to Romans 5:5 as a key text here, where "the love of God" is "poured into our hearts" by the Spirit. Here, he thought, is the key to the divine reordering of human affections: that the Spirit pours *a love for God* into the human heart. Augustine takes the genitive in ἡ ἀγάπη τοῦ θεοῦ ("the love of God") as grammatically "objective": human love toward God is made the referent. This reading of the verse is fundamental to Augustine's account of how the Spirit reorders our affections, yet most now agree that Augustine misread the verse.[36] Does this exegetical problem constitute a fatal blow to his account of how the Spirit reorders the affections?

Not at all. The verse functions as a slogan for what can be easily derived from elsewhere in the Bible.[37] Augustine celebrates the God of Psalm 36, the lavishly proactive lover of humanity who pours his own boundless love out upon his people, and where a string of metaphors, including feasting at God's banquet and drinking at his fountain, picture people in helpless response.[38] The Spirit works in us a joining of loves — a fitting response to the God whose ardent love Isaiah describes in a most startling simile, using the language of a wedding night: that just "as the bridegroom rejoices over the bride, so shall your God rejoice over you" (Isa. 62:5).[39] The Spirit reorders our affections to respond in joy to his divine and holy affection.

---

36. Despite ἐκκέχυται, Augustine's exegesis is hard to defend in context, since the point of the text is to give assurance of hope despite tribulation. Therefore the majority reading is of a "subjective" genitive, with God's own love toward people on view. For a straightforward exposition along these lines, see, e.g., C. E. B. Cranfield, *A Critical and Exegetical Commentary on the Epistle to the Romans (I-VIII)* 2 vols., vol. 1 (Edinburgh: T. & T. Clark, 1975), p. 262, n. 2. But on Romans 15:30, Cranfield can argue *against* a subjective genitive (the Spirit's love toward humanity), and for a genitive of origin (C. E. B. Cranfield, *A Critical and Exegetical Commentary on the Epistle to the Romans [IX-XVI]*, 2 vols., vol. 2 [Edinburgh: T. & T. Clark, 1979], p. 776, n. 2). There is nothing to be gained by mounting a technical challenge of Augustine's theologically astute "eisegesis" of Romans 5:5.

37. E.g., Rom. 15:30; Gal. 5:22; Col. 1:8; or 2 Tim. 1:7.

38. Augustine, *On the Spirit and the Letter*, passim.

39. I owe this insight into Isaiah 62–63, and its relevance to my argument, to Rev. Dr. Richard Gibson. We should also remember the New Testament's equally audacious representation of the Lord Christ as a bridegroom who joyously awaits his wedding day to his bride, the church (Rev. 19:7-8; 21:5, 9; cf. Eph. 5:23-24, 29, 32).

c) Love Commended

But what can be said for those who have not yet experienced this reordering? Augustine speaks of our "flight" to God: a movement of dependence and humility, spoken in prayer.[40] Augustine does not wish this "flight" to be misunderstood as being particularly difficult. The *Confessions* show it worked out in one man's life, and although there is mystery about what triggers the flight and how it can proceed in obsessive, distracted humans, whoever takes and reads the *Confessions* can find themselves doing as Augustine did and praying as he prays. Augustine also points to the experience of the sports stadium. He reminds the (apparently young male) listeners of what comes over them there. Simply by watching their friends, and attending to the action, a deep love for the sportsmen and the sport grows. Though mysterious, this process is also quite accessible.[41]

Hence there is no embarrassment for Augustine in *commending* and even in gently *commanding* love. In this context the specification of "love" is narrowed to denote its proper object, the "perfectly ordered and harmonious enjoyment of God and of one another in God."[42] Augustine suggests that we aim toward these new loves, as opposed to our obsessional loves. Love can be commended in this way on the understanding that the mysterious changes are themselves divinely gifted. By enjoining his hearers to engage in love for God and for others, Augustine understands people simply to be finding the correct response to the reality already before them, but from which they have been distracted by their obsessions.

He even suggests that we should aim at loving this love itself: "It is by love that other things come to be rightly loved; then how must itself be loved!"[43] Although Augustine is riskily abstract here, his commendation remains more apposite than ever. To a culture like ours, given to anomie

---

40. Augustine, *On the Spirit and the Letter*, 105-6 (§51).

41. Brown, *Augustine* (new ed.), pp. 448-49.

42. Or near equivalent — twice in *City of God* XIX.13 and once in XIX.17. Cf. Oliver M. T. O'Donovan, "Augustinian Ethics," in *A New Dictionary of Christian Ethics*, ed. James F. Childress and John Macquarrie (London: SCM, 1986); and Oliver M. T. O'Donovan, *The Problem of Self-Love in St. Augustine* (New Haven and London: Yale University Press, 1980), p. 25.

43. Augustine, *Homilies on the First Epistle of John*, ed. Philip Schaff, trans. H. Browne, *NPNF 1*, vol. 7 (Grand Rapids: Eerdmans, 1986; originally published New York, 1888), p. 501 (VII.1).

and despair, Augustine might say that although our life in the world is like a desert wandering, love "is the fountain which God has been pleased to place here" to sustain our journey.[44]

6. The Consolation of New Treasures

C. S. Lewis has an Augustinian view of the way all of our obsessions are mere glimpses of our proper home.

> Our Lord finds our desires not too strong, but too weak. We are half-hearted creatures, fooling about with drink and sex and ambition when infinite joy is offered us, like an ignorant child who wants to go on making mud pies in a slum because he cannot imagine what is meant by the offer of a holiday at the sea. We are far too easily pleased.[45]

Augustine points us to the proper object of our love, so that old treasures we obsessed about can fall away as boring, or find their proper place. The treasure of heaven becomes the treasure of our hearts, as we willingly sell everything else to possess that pearl (Matt. 6:19-21; Luke 12:31-34; Matt. 13:45-46).

Until then, we are consoled at first when we rest safely in Christ, even in the grip of our obsessing weakness; then, under the gentle power of the Spirit, flying to God in prayer, and aiming for new loves. We find ourselves responding to his own passionate love, and are then stirred to a new love for others and a proper love of the created order.

Perhaps Augustine's psychology is at its greatest in his famous statement to God: "you have made us for yourself, O Lord, and our hearts" — our obsessive hearts, we might say — "find no peace until they rest in you."[46]

---

44. Augustine, *Homilies*, p. 501 (VII.1).

45. C. S. Lewis, "The Weight of Glory," in *The Weight of Glory*, ed. Walter Hooper (London: HarperCollins, 1976), p. 16.

46. Augustine, *Conf.*, p. 21 (I.1).

Bibliography

[Author unnamed]. "Terms of Enjoyment." *Reader's Digest* October 2005. Online: http://www.rd.com/content/openContent.do?contentId=28679&pageIndex=0 (accessed 19/9/2006).

Augustine. *The City of God Against the Pagans.* Translated by R. W. Dyson. *Cambridge Texts in the History of Political Thought* edition. Cambridge: Cambridge University Press, 1998.

———. *Confessions.* Translated by R. S. Pine-Coffin. *Penguin Classics* edition. Harmondsworth: Penguin, 1961.

———. *Homilies on the First Epistle of John.* Edited by Philip Schaff. Translated by H. Browne. *NPNF* 1, vol. 7. Grand Rapids: Eerdmans, 1986. Originally published New York, 1888.

———. *On the Spirit and the Letter.* Edited by Philip Schaff. Translated by Peter Holmes and Robert E. Wallis. *NPNF* 1, vol. 5. Grand Rapids: Eerdmans, 1987. Originally published New York, 1887.

Brown, Peter. *Augustine of Hippo: A Biography (A New Edition with an Epilogue).* London: Faber, 2000.

Cranfield, C. E. B. *A Critical and Exegetical Commentary on the Epistle to the Romans (I-VIII).* 2 vols., vol. 1. Edinburgh: T. & T. Clark, 1975.

———. *A Critical and Exegetical Commentary on the Epistle to the Romans (IX-XVI).* 2 vols., vol. 2. Edinburgh: T. & T. Clark, 1979.

Dixon, Thomas. "Theology, Anti-Theology and Atheology: From Christian Passions to Secular Emotions," *Modern Theology* 15, no. 3 (1999): 297-330.

Griffiths, Paul E. *What Emotions Really Are: The Problem of Psychological Categories.* Chicago: University of Chicago Press, 1997.

Hastings, James, ed. *Encyclopaedia of Religion and Ethics.* Vol. 7 (Hymns-Liberty). Edinburgh: T. & T. Clark, 1914.

Haykin, Michael A. G. *Eminent Christians: 12. Augustine of Hippo.* Online: http://mghhistor.blogspot.com/2006/09/eminent-christians-augustine-of-hippo.html (accessed 19/09/2006).

Lawson, Amy. "Sun Addicts Need AA-Type Program," *The Sunday Age* 2 October 2005.

Lewis, C. S. "The Weight of Glory." In *The Weight of Glory,* edited by Walter Hooper, pp. 25-46. London: HarperCollins, 1976.

Miles, Margaret R. *Augustine on the Body,* vol. 31. Missoula: Scholars Press, 1979.

O'Donovan, Oliver M. T. "Augustinian Ethics." In *A New Dictionary of Chris-*

tian Ethics, edited by James F. Childress and John Macquarrie, p. 46. London: SCM, 1986.

———. *The Problem of Self-Love in St. Augustine.* New Haven and London: Yale University Press, 1980.

Outler, Albert C., ed. *Augustine: Confessions and Enchiridion.* Vol. 7, *Library of Christian Classics.* London: SCM Press, 1955. Online: http://www.fordham.edu/halsall/basis/confessions-bod.html (accessed 13/5/2006).

Taylor, Charles. *Sources of the Self: The Making of the Modern Identity.* Cambridge: Cambridge University Press, 1989.

LUTHER
on Despair

MARK D. THOMPSON

Though the fig tree does not bud
*   and there are no grapes on the vines,*
though the olive crop fails
*   and the fields produce no food,*
though there are no sheep in the pen
*   and no cattle in the stalls,*
yet will I rejoice in the LORD,
*   I will be joyful in God my Savior.*

Habakkuk 3:17-18

It is one of the perverse contradictions of our time that so much effort has been expended to make life carefree and enjoyable and yet still for very many all that life seems to offer is the grinding sense of being utterly lost, an overpowering conviction that there is no way forward and no way out. For many, despair is the emotion that sums up life at the beginning of this new millennium. There is no hope, nothing ahead but emptiness and ruin. Every path has been blocked and all prospect of peace, security, and of joy is gone. Despair reflects the ultimate disempowerment.

Too many people know despair from the inside. Of course not every experience of despair is the same. Despair comes in many forms and has just as many causes. For some its causes are biological or chemical and its treatment is best sought through the expertise of the medical profession.

For others the causes are circumstances, or perceptions of circumstances that drain the joy and resilience of the individual until nothing seems left but darkness. For still others despair is something that rushes upon them like a violent attacker determined to cut them down for unknown reasons. Despair, it seems, refuses to be straightjacketed.

Despair has echoed with increasing volume through the popular expressions of our culture over the last two hundred years. The despairing individual, head buried in his or her hands, has been a long-standing interest of sculptors and painters. Poets have sought to give it voice, as in T. S. Eliot's famous poem "The Wasteland," worked into shape during his own recovery from a nervous breakdown in 1921:

> On Margate Sands
> I can connect
> Nothing with nothing.
> The broken fingernails of dirty hands.
> My people humble people who expect
> Nothing.

It appears repeatedly as a theme in the lyrics of popular songs and ballads in a wide variety of genres. Whether it be "Terrapin Station" by the Grateful Dead,[1] or Tina Arena's "The Machine's Breaking Down,"[2] or the slower, more haunting "Another Day in Paradise" by Genesis,[3] they all seek to convey a sense of emptiness and the loss of hope that echoes what so many feel. Despair resonates. We can imagine what it would be like to be there.

But perhaps the most powerful image of despair at the beginning of

1. "Inspiration, move me brightly. Light the song with sense and color; Hold away despair, more than this I will not ask. Faced with mysteries dark and vast, statements just seem vain at last. . . . While you were gone, these faces filled with darkness. The obvious was hidden. With nothing to believe in . . ." "Terrapin Station," lyrics by Robert Hunter, music by Jerry Garcia.

2. "Addicts bent on self-destruction/A billion dollars for the masters of seduction/Despair and hope go hand in hand/Charting the inevitable course of man/Bloody images bounce off the wall/As the satellite pictures tell it all/While common goals and common ground/Disappear as the world breaks down. . . ." "The Machine's Breaking Down," lyrics by Tina Arena, music by Ross Inglis.

3. "She calls out to the man on the street/Sir, can you help me?/It's cold and I've nowhere to sleep/Is there somewhere you can tell me?/He walks on, doesn't look back/He pretends he can't hear her/Starts to whistle as he crosses the street/Seems embarrassed to be there . . ." "Another Day in Paradise," lyrics and music by Phil Collins.

the twenty-first century is not found in art, or literature, or even popular music. It is found in a single photograph. The picture now known to the world simply as "The Falling Man" was taken at 9:41 A.M. on 11 September 2001 by Richard Drew, a photographer working for the Associated Press. If you've ever seen it you won't have forgotten it. It shows a single man falling from high in the North Tower of the World Trade Center less than an hour after American Airlines Flight 11 crashed into it. The quiet dignity of that man's fall to his death has never obscured the horror and tragedy of the moment. Nor has it diminished our sense of the desperate choice he faced. There *was* no way out for the falling man. All hope *was* gone. Only forty-seven minutes later the entire North Tower, once 110 stories tall, would collapse.

Strangely enough, some have argued in the last few years that the perpetrators of that suffering in September 2001 were themselves the victims of despair. The *Independent,* a British newspaper, carried this headline on 25 March 2002: "Suicide bombers are the appalling but inevitable result of decades of despair."[4] This horrific phenomenon has arisen, so the argument goes, because these young men and women can see no way ahead, no hope for peace or security in a world seduced into accepting a blatant double standard on terror. When no one will listen and the number of the dead among their own people seems to grow exponentially, what is left but this last frantic effort to make the West sit up and take notice of what they have done to the Middle East? Despair can paralyze. It can bring you to the point of giving up altogether. But it can also force you to the most extreme measures.

At this point we are not all that far from the controversial suggestion of the early twentieth-century sociologist Emile Durkheim (1858-1917), who found one explanation for the phenomenon of suicide in the condition he labeled *anomie.* When society fails to impose external limits on the passions and appetites of individuals, human beings tend to aspire to everything and are satisfied with nothing. "Man is the more vulnerable to self-destruction," Durkheim wrote, "the more he is detached from any collectivity, that is to say, the more he lives as an egoist." As a contemporary commentator summarizes: "Out of disillusionment and despair with the

---

4. Sa'id Ghazali, "Suicide bombers are the inevitable result of decades of despair," *Independent* 25 March 2002. Online at http://comment.independent.co.uk/commentators/article194229.ece

pursuit of limitless goals, many individuals in the anomic society take their own lives."[5] It is not just those who are trapped who experience despair. The libertarian revolutions have their costs as well.

But there is another kind of despair I have not yet touched upon. We might call it "despair in a spiritual key," that sense of being abandoned by God himself, of being condemned with no way out because God has set himself up as your enemy. It can arise from an acute sense of our failure to live up to even our own standards of behavior, let alone those of God. It can be intensified by a narrow focus on the justice of God and the necessity of a decisive judgment against all wrongdoing. Alternatively, it can be the product of circumstances that scream out that God is not on your side. Classic expressions of despair in this sense have been detected in a number of the psalms of the Old Testament, for example:

> My God, my God, why have you forsaken me?
>> Why are you so far from saving me,
>> from the words of my groaning?
> O my God, I cry by day, but you do not answer,
>> and by night, but I find no rest. (Ps. 22:1-2)

> You have put me in the lowest pit,
>> in the darkest depths.
> Your wrath lies heavily upon me;
>> you have overwhelmed me with all your waves.
> You have taken from me my closest friends
>> and have made me repulsive to them.
> I am confined and cannot escape;
>> my eyes are dim with grief. . . .
> Why, O LORD, do you reject me
>> and hide your face from me? (Ps. 88:6-9a, 14)

Such cries of despair are found on the lips of the prophets as well. The prophet Jeremiah laments, "the Lord has become like an enemy" (Lam. 2:5). Habakkuk piles up one protest upon another as he is overwhelmed with grief at the fate of his people:

5. Emile Durkheim, *Suicide: A Study in Sociology,* trans. John A. Spaulding and George Simpson (Glencoe, Ill.: Free Press, 1951 [French original 1930]), p. 271; Durkheim 1972, p. 113; J. Orcutt, *Analyzing Deviance* (Homewood, Ill.: Dorsey, 1983), p. 68.

How long, O LORD, must I call for help,
    but you do not listen?
Or cry out to you, "Violence!"
    but you do not save?
Why do you make me look at injustice?
    Why do you tolerate wrong?
Destruction and violence are before me;
    there is strife, and conflict abounds.
Therefore the law is paralyzed,
    and justice never prevails.
The wicked hem in the righteous
    so that justice is perverted. (Hab. 1:2-4)

It is evident from just this brief glance that despair is a complex phenomenon. It is not susceptible to simple definition; its causes are varied and in some cases multiple. This alone should caution us against facile suggestions for how it might be overcome. Care must be taken to identify the nature and the cause of each particular instance of despair and to respond appropriately. Nevertheless, there is a common element to despair in each of the modes we have discussed so far: *despair is the loss of all hope,* hope for a change in circumstances, hope for a share of peace and happiness, hope for mercy and forgiveness.

Has Christian theology anything to say to those trapped in the downward spiral of despair? Is there a secure basis for hope that can be given to those who have lost all hope? Christians approach these questions in the expectation that there is. After all, Christian theology is at its heart talk about God, the God who not only created humanity in the first place but who entered into it and took to himself our fragile and broken nature in order to restore us to himself. Our despair and its causes are not unknown to the living God. Nor have those who have known God through the centuries been strangers to times of frustration, betrayal, hopelessness, and despair. Yet they found in the rich storehouse of Christian doctrine, not a quick fix, but resources that, particularly in those cases where despair has a spiritual dimension, can lift the oppressive blanket of hopelessness and bring light where there has been only darkness.

One man who knew all about doubt and struggle and despair was the German Reformer, Martin Luther (1483-1546). He even coined a term for the black periods he experienced so often: they were his *Anfechtungen.*

Sometimes the darkness would last for days, or even weeks. He never minimized the seriousness of these "assaults" or "trials" (the German word is translated in a number of ways and probably should remain untranslated), but he learned to view them differently, not as experiences to be endured but as opportunities to be embraced.

Martin Luther: The Man Who Knew Despair

Martin Luther had never intended to become a monk, let alone a university lecturer in theology. Yet on 2 July 1505 the course of his life was changed as a result of terror. Caught in a thunderstorm just outside of Stotternheim and fearing for his life, Luther vowed that if he was spared he would become a monk. Conscientious in a way that many in our cynical age find difficult to understand, Luther insisted on keeping his vow and entered the famed order of Observant Augustinians before the month was over.

Life among the Augustinian friars was hard, but then life in general was hard in the sixteenth century. If anything, the scholarly environment of the cloister gave Luther opportunities to develop his intellectual gifts that were rare in other settings. It was not so much the rigor of the daily routine or the intellectual demands of his order that made these years so difficult for Luther. Rather, Luther was repeatedly brought low by his own sensitive conscience. The same conscience that ensured he kept his vow back in 1505 kept exposing his failure to live as the law of God demanded.

The result was a vivid sense of being abandoned by God or, more accurately, of standing under the terrifying wrath of God the righteous judge. The experience was, for Luther, nothing short of torture. In what is clearly an autobiographical note from 1518, which he deliberately shaped along the lines of the Apostle Paul's comment in 2 Corinthians 12, Luther recalled:

> I myself knew a man who claimed that he had often suffered these punishments, and in fact over a very brief period of time. Yet they were so great and so much like hell that no tongue could adequately express them, no pen could describe them, and no one who had not himself experienced them could believe them. And so great were they that, if they had been sustained or had lasted for half an hour, even for one-tenth of an hour, he would have perished completely and all of his bones would have been reduced to ashes. At such a time God seems so terribly angry,

and with him the whole creation. At such a time there is no flight, no comfort, within or without, but all things accuse. At such a time as that the Psalmist mourns, "I am cut off from thy sight," or at least he does not dare to say "O Lord . . . do not chasten me in thy wrath." In this moment (strange to say) the soul cannot believe that it can ever be redeemed other than that the punishment is not yet completely felt.[6]

Luther was not alone in this struggle, a point that is sometimes missed by his modern and postmodern critics.[7] Indeed the monks had a name for the experience: "the bath of Satan." Immersed in guilt, those so afflicted would often be driven to doubt God's willingness to be merciful. As a result the experience itself was considered sinful, and the *Skrupulant*, as such a person would be labeled, was caught further in a downward spiral of anguish and despair.[8]

Yet even within the structures of monastic life there were attempts to provide consolation for those who found themselves plagued in this way. The sacrament of penance is the most obvious case in point. A monk's confession of sin to a designated father confessor, combined with genuine contrition, would be met with the words of absolution and an opportunity for satisfaction. We know that Luther and his contemporaries made frequent use of the confessional. "We exhausted our confessors," he would remember later.[9] Indeed, he recalled spending six hours with his father confessor on one occasion.[10]

Nevertheless, whatever the intention, the experience of confession could itself be a harrowing one, as confessional manuals from the period

---

6. *Explanation of the Ninety-five Theses* (1518) *WA* I, 557.33-558.3 = *LW* 31, 129.

7. "Standing in fear of the judgment of God was not the innovation of an obscure monk in the sixteenth century. Luther's perceptions of sin may have been more intense than was customary, but they were far from new" (J. von Rohr, "Medieval Consolation and the Young Luther's Despair," in *Reformation Studies: Essays in Honor of Roland H. Bainton*, ed. Franklin H. Littell [Richmond: John Knox, 1962], p. 64). Rohr points to Jean Gerson as one who understood the kind of despair that Luther experienced. *De remedies contra pusillanimitatem*, III, 585C. See also H. A. Oberman, *Luther: Man Between God and the Devil*, trans. Eileen Walliser-Schwarzbart (New Haven: Yale University Press, 1989 [German original 1982]), p. 177 and W. Dress, "Gerson und Luther," *Zeitschrift für Kirchengeschichte* 52 (1933): 122-61.

8. M. Brecht, *Martin Luther: His Road to Reformation 1483-1521*, trans. James L. Schaaf (Minneapolis: Fortress, 1985 [German original 1981]), p. 80.

9. *Commentary on Psalm 51 WA* XL-II, 317.29-30; #4362 *WATr* IV, 260.36-261.6 = *LW* 54, 334; #6017 *WATr* V, 439.32-440.22.

10. *WA* XV, 489.3.

testify.[11] First, there was the need for *thoroughness* in giving an account of your sins. Luther would often be plagued with the doubt that "you left this out of your confession," or "you did not do that properly."[12] Then there was the requirement for *contrition*, not merely a remorse arising out of fear of punishment, but a genuine sorrow arising out of love for God and a concern for his honor. Here, too, Luther was plagued with the accusation of his own conscience: "You have not been properly contrite."[13] Could it be that his self-loathing was merely the device of sophisticated self-interest? Finally, there was the necessity of *satisfaction*, typically the last thing the penitent heard in the process of confession. Luther wore himself out with acts of satisfaction but found no peace in them because he could never be sure he had done enough or that what he had done was done properly.[14] Undoubtedly Luther was unusually sensitive at each of these points. However, there is evidence that his problems were by no means unique and that the real cause was the legalistic framework in which this opportunity for consolation was presented.[15] There were always requirements, preconditions, and consequential actions, which meant the penitent was continually thrown back on his own capacity to perform. Where the necessary standard was not attained, judgment remained inevitable.

Luther's superiors appear to have shown particular care for their troubled young colleague. They devised ways of occupying his intellectual energy, giving him the task of memorizing Scripture and enrolling him in advanced theological studies. In 1512 he took over from his father confessor as a member of the theology faculty at the relatively new university in Wittenberg. It was there by the river Elbe that Luther famously made his discovery. Sitting at his desk, poring over the epistle of Paul to the Romans in preparation for his lectures, he came to understand that God's righteousness is not merely his just punishment of sinners, but a gift he bestows on those who have faith in Christ.[16] In his own words from much later,

11. S. E. Ozment, *The Reformation in the Cities: The Appeal of Protestantism to Sixteenth-Century Germany and Switzerland* (New Haven: Yale University Press, 1975), pp. 23-26.

12. #6669 *WATr* VI, 106.32-107.3.

13. *WA* XL XL-II, 15.19-20 = *LW* 27, 13.

14. *WA* XLIV, 819.10-16 = *LW* 8, 326.

15. Rohr, "Medieval Consolation and the Young Luther's Despair," pp. 64-67.

16. Taking their cue from some comments amidst Luther's famous *Table Talk*, in which he speaks of this discovery being made while he was *in cloaca* (literally, "on the toilet"), many have attempted to make connections between Luther's physical and psychological ailments and his

I had indeed been captivated with an extraordinary ardor for understanding Paul in the Epistle to the Romans. But up till then it was not the cold blood about the heart, but a single word in Chapter 1, "In it the righteousness of God is revealed," that had stood in my way. For I hated that word "righteousness of God," which, according to the use and custom of all the teachers, I had been taught to understand philosophically regarding the formal or active righteousness, as they called it, with which God is righteous and punishes the unrighteous sinner.

Though I lived as a monk without reproach, I felt that I was a sinner before God with an extremely disturbed conscience. I could not believe that he was placated by my satisfaction. I did not love, yes, I hated the righteous God who punishes sinners, and secretly, if not blasphemously, certainly murmuring greatly, I was angry with God, and said, "As if, indeed, it is not enough, that miserable sinners, eternally lost through original sin, are crushed by every kind of calamity by the law of the Ten Commandments, without having God add pain to pain by the gospel and also by the gospel threatening us with his righteousness and wrath!" Thus I raged with a fierce and troubled conscience. Nevertheless, I beat importunately upon Paul at that place, most ardently desiring to know what St. Paul wanted.

At last, by the mercy of God, meditating day and night, I gave heed to the context of the words, namely, "In it the righteousness of God is revealed, as it is written, 'He who through faith is righteous shall live.'" There I began to understand that the righteousness of God is that by which the righteous lives by a gift of God, namely by faith. And this is the meaning: the righteousness of God is revealed by the gospel, namely, the passive righteousness with which merciful God justifies us by faith, as it is written, "He who through faith is righteous shall live." Here I felt that I was altogether born again and had entered paradise itself through open gates. There a totally other face of the entire Scripture showed itself to me.[17]

---

new theology. However, we do know that Luther's heated study room was in the cloaca tower in the monastery at Wittenberg and so the reference need not be taken as literally as many have done with great relish. As Martin Brecht summarizes, "No matter how much the conception of Luther making his reformatory discovery while on the privy may accord with the fantasies of polemicists, psychologists, and even theologians, it is really much more probable that he attained his insight at his desk while about his exegetical work" (Brecht 1985, p. 227).

17. *Foreword to the first volume of the Collected Latin Works* (1545) *WA* 54, 185.14-186.10 = *LW* 34, 336-37.

Luther's discovery, or "recovery" as he would have called it, was revolutionary. It transformed his own life as it would transform the lives of millions of others in the centuries that followed. No longer was his *performance* the critical factor. Acceptance by God, forgiveness, and the life of righteousness were all a *gift* of God secured by the life, death, and resurrection of Jesus, not by anything we have achieved or might achieve in the future. The righteousness of God was good news once more.

In the wake of this insight Luther would oppose the system that had long obscured and even contradicted this wonderfully liberating truth. His two great disputations from the year 1517, *Against Scholastic Theology* and *Against the Power of Indulgences* (the "Ninety-five theses"), placed Luther at the center of massive religious upheaval. In the months that followed, he could not keep up with the demand for explanations of the faith in the light of discoveries he had made. His books were being read throughout Europe. Some hailed him as a hero. Others wrote their own more critical responses. The protest of one little German monk was snowballing into a movement that would reshape Christendom. Before long Luther would be condemned by a papal proclamation. Then he would be forced to answer before the Holy Roman Emperor and the representatives of the Pope at the Diet of Worms in April 1521. In the wake of that appearance and in order to protect Luther, his own prince, Elector Frederick the Wise, engineered a kidnapping, and for ten months he was kept under guard in the Wartburg, a castle fortress just outside of Eisenach. There is most certainly a heroic dimension to the Luther story in these years. Here was a great defender of freedom and truth. Here was a man willing to stand against the most powerful religious and political authorities of the time for the sake of truth. "Here I stand, I cannot do otherwise, God help me. Amen."[18]

But the recovery of the apostolic perspective that we are set right with God by Christ's work rather than our own and that we receive this great benefit by faith did not bring an end to Luther's experiences of despair. At Worms he was hailed as a hero but assailed by doubts and despair when alone in his room. At the Wartburg he railed at the devil who assaulted him in this way with shouts so loud that the regular occupants of the castle wondered what was going on. And yet the assaults kept coming. Luther remained conscious of his own failures and weakness. However, these doubts

---

18. The reported words that ended Luther's speech at Worms, but that do not appear on the official record. *WA* VII, 838.9 = *LW* 32, 113.

and trials now also had another focus. Alongside the old questions were new ones like "Are you really the only wise man?" and "Look what *you* have unleashed. What if you are simply leading all these people down to the pit of hell with you?"[19]

Those years were not without moments of joy and triumph. In June 1525 Luther married Katherine von Bora, one of those who had fled the nunnery at Nimbschen more than two years earlier. Though hardly a Hollywood romance, their union was not a passionless commitment to duty either. The letters they wrote to each other testify that Luther deeply loved his "Katie" and she was devoted to him.[20] But Katie had to contend with her husband's regular bouts of despair. Luther made no secret of them; he wrote of them regularly in his letters.[21] On 2 August 1527 he wrote to Melanchthon, pulling no punches:

> For the last week I have been thrown into hell and the pit, my whole body so bruised that I still tremble in all my members. I had almost lost Christ and was thrown to the billows and buffeted by storms of despair so that I was tempted to blaspheme against God.[22]

Yet it was Katie who saw him at his worst: locked in his room for days at a time or unable to get out of bed.

Luther's later life also included opportunities for him to care for others who suffered as he regularly did. The prominence of the *Anfechtungen* in his table discussions of the 1530s may at least partly be explained by the fact that during these years the Luthers were host to Jerome Weller and Johann Schlaginhaufen, two students who both suffered from depression.[23] At the same time Luther regularly traveled to Dessau to act as pas-

---

19. *The Misuse of the Mass* (1521) *WA* VIII, 482.32-483.8 = *LW* 36, 134. See M. D. Thompson, *A Sure Ground on Which to Stand: The Relation Between Authority and Interpretive Method in Luther's Approach to Scripture* (Carlisle: Paternoster, 2002), pp. 209-10.

20. E.g., (5 June 1530) *WABr* V, 347-48 = *LW* 49, 312-16; (15 August 1530) *WABr* V, 545-46 = *LW* 49, 401-2; (27 February 1532) *WABr* VI, 270-71 = *LW* 50, 48-50; (29 July 1534) *WABr* VII, 91 = *LW* 50, 80-81; (2 July 1540) *WABr* IX, 168 = *LW* 50, 208-12.

21. Over the next two decades Luther wrote regularly to his friend at the Electoral court, Georg Spalatin. Mentions of Luther's ongoing *Anfechtungen* loom large in that correspondence, e.g., (21 March 1537) *WABr* VIII, 59 = *LW* 50, 170.

22. *Luther to Melanchthon* (2 August 1527) *WABr* IV, 226.9-11.

23. M. Brecht, *Martin Luther: Shaping and Defining the Reformation 1521-1532*, trans. James L. Schaaf (Minneapolis: Fortress, 1990 [German original 1986]), pp. 378-79; M. Brecht,

tor to Prince Joachim I of Anhalt-Dessau, who likewise had an ongoing struggle with depression.[24] Luther had long known that his experience of despair was not unique, but these pastoral opportunities gave him even greater cause to analyze the *Anfechtungen* in terms of general principles and practical advice. There is some evidence that Luther sought out those who suffered in this way in order to care for them.[25]

A Clear View of the Nature of Despair

Luther refused to hide the reality of his ongoing struggle with despair. He was never interested in a triumphalist picture of the Christian life that itself could be a snare for those who suffered in one way or another. In fact, he was increasingly concerned as the years rolled by to stress the normality of the experience of assault, trial, and suffering. This is precisely what we ought to expect if we are to live as true disciples of Christ. Early on, in 1519, he spoke of how the example of Christ enduring Godforsakenness for us and being tempted to the extreme yet remaining faithful should give an entirely new perspective to our own struggles. These are not just things to be endured, they are opportunities to be conformed to Christ.[26] Ten years later, in his *Greater Catechism,* Luther spoke of how spiritual distress and temptation are unavoidable in this life: "No one can avoid temptation and enticement as long as we live in the flesh and have the devil around us; and this will not change: we must bear tribulation, yes even be in the midst of it. But that is why we pray not to fall into and drown in it. That is why it is different to feel spiritual distress than to accept temptation and say 'yes' to it."[27] In the early 1530s Luther spoke in even stronger terms to those who gathered around his table: "If I should live a little while longer, I would like to write a book about *Anfechtung.* Without it no man can rightly understand the Holy Scriptures or know what the fear and love of God is all about. In fact, without *Anfechtung* one does not really know what the spiritual life is."[28]

Martin Luther: The Preservation of the Church 1532-1546, trans. James L. Schaaf (Minneapolis: Fortress, 1993 [German original 1987]), pp. 129-30.

24. Brecht 1993, pp. 27-28.
25. Brecht 1993, p. 255.
26. WA II, 141.8, 690.17, 691.23.
27. *Greater Catechism* (1529) WA XXX-I, 209.24-28.
28. #4777 (1530) WA Tr IV, 490.24-491.1.

Despair never ceases to be despair. The dark periods may well be horrific and prolonged. That certainly was Luther's own experience. At such times nothing is to be gained by minimizing the seriousness of what is happening. However, Luther insisted that it was important to understand that this is not a sign of God's displeasure or condemnation. The lies at the heart of this experience must not be believed. As he wrote around 1528,

> When God sends us tribulation Satan suggests: See there, God flings you into prison and endangers your life. Surely He hates you. He is angry with you; for if He did not hate you, He would not allow this thing to happen. In this way Satan turns the rod of a Father into the rope of a hangman and the most salutary remedy into the deadliest poison. But he is an incredible master at devising thoughts of this nature.[29]

It is the gospel, the promise anchored in the death and resurrection of Jesus, that shows us this simply is not so. God has another, better purpose just as the sufferings of Christ led to victory and rich blessing. The trials experienced by the Christian are "not evil but good imposed by a good God."[30] Commenting on Psalm 51 in 1538 Luther insisted,

> We have to learn that a Christian should walk in the midst of death, in the remorse and trembling of his conscience, in the midst of the devil's teeth and of hell, and yet should keep the Word of grace, so that in much trembling we say, "You, O Lord, do look on me with favour."[31]

Luther does not always make a clear distinction between the despair caused by the tender conscience and that caused by circumstances such as physical illness, the loss of a loved one, or the assault of an enemy.[32] The stress of engaging in controversy with Zwingli and others at Marburg in 1529 merged seamlessly into another round of *Anfechtung* for Luther. In later life his various physical ailments seemed regularly to be accompanied by the inward spiritual struggle to trust and to resist temptation. The explanation for the way these things come together so often in Luther's letters and table conver-

---

29. *Lectures on Isaiah* (1527-29) *WA* XXV, 179.14-19. This quote is from the older edition of notes from Luther's lectures from the hand of Antonius Lauterbach.

30. *Lectures on Isaiah* (1527-29) *WA* XXXI-II, 152.14 = *LW* 16, 214.

31. *Commentary on Psalm 51:17* (1538) *WA* XL-II, 462.17-20 = *LW* 12, 405.

32. P. T. Bühler, *Die Anfechtung bei Martin Luther* (Zurich: Zwingli-Verlag, 1942), p. 28; Brecht 1990, p. 207.

sation seems to be that, in Luther's mind at least, all of them were in fact aspects of the same phenomenon. The brokenness of discipleship in between Jesus' resurrection and his return has many dimensions.

Anfechtung need not be simply the private burden of individuals either. Strife within the churches, public opposition to the ministers or those preparing to be ministers, the emergence of fanaticism and heresies, and the prolonged enmity of the pope and those commissioned by him — all these were part of the assault Christians are to bear. "There is no church without the cross and *Anfechtung*."[33] The church, like the Christian, lives under the shadow of the cross and in a broken world. Indeed, so convinced is Luther that these struggles are "a characteristic condition of the Christian life," that he suggests we should be more concerned when they are not experienced than when they are. It is no surprise then that, when the fanatical Zwickau prophets arrived in Wittenberg in 1522, claiming they had new messages for the people direct from God himself, Luther should instruct Melanchthon to inquire of them about their own experience of struggle and defeat:

> In order to explore their individual spirit, too, you should inquire whether they have experienced spiritual distress and the divine birth, death and hell. If you should hear that all [their experiences] are pleasant, quiet, devout (as they say), and spiritual, then don't approve of them, even if they should say that they were caught up to the third heaven. The sign of the Son of Man is then missing, which is the only touchstone of Christians and a certain differentiator between the spirits.[34]

Struggle is a sign of life; indeed it is a sign of a genuine intersection of the work of God and the brokenness or hostility of the world. Where it is absent, questions need to be asked. For "it nearly always happens that those who should be frightened are most complacent and, on the other hand, that those who are in need of comfort feel anguish and despair."[35] Here is the paradox at the heart of the Christian self-perception:

> A godly man feels sin more than grace, wrath more than favour, judgment more than redemption. An ungodly man feels almost no wrath,

---

33. Brecht 1993, p. 190; see also J. W. Kleinig, "Oratio, Meditatio, Tentatio: What Makes a Theologian?," *Concordia Theological Quarterly* 66, no. 3 (2002): 264.

34. *Letter to Philip Melanchthon* (13 January 1522) *WABr* II, 425.22-27 = *LW* 48, 366.

35. *Commentary on Genesis 19:23-25* (1537) *WA* XLIII, 85.25-26 = *LW* 3, 293-94.

but is smug as though there were no wrath anywhere, as though there were no God anywhere who vindicates His righteousness. This happens mostly in those who strive for some appearance of religion.[36]

For Luther, acknowledging the reality of the human struggle with hopelessness and despair, in particular the Christian's ongoing struggle with these things, was a critical first step in providing genuine consolation for those in the midst of it. Luther expected daily Christian living to be shaped by the pattern of Jesus' suffering, just as a true knowledge of God and a proper perspective on the church must also be determined by the cross of Christ. Luther's theology is in very large measure a *theologia crucis,* a theology of the cross. In an important sense, the struggle for hope in the midst of darkness is its existential edge.

Luther had no trouble in attributing the *Anfechtungen* to the work of God in his life. They are God's instruments to strengthen faith, to cause us to abandon our self-reliance and trust in Christ alone. In an important sense we *must* despair of all else in order to wholeheartedly rely on Christ and what he has accomplished for us.[37] This perspective is deeply rooted in the wider contours of Luther's thought. God is about rescuing men and women. That is his preoccupation, his "proper work" *(opus proprium Dei)*. However, these assaults from various sources, the *Anfechtungen,* are part of a strange work of God *(opus alienum Dei)*, which brings us low and so serves the interests of God's proper work. God undermines our pride and self-confidence in order that we might take seriously our ongoing need of forgiveness and mercy. By this struggle God nourishes faith.[38] Realizing this proper context for the assaults that plague him, Luther is even able to rejoice in them.[39]

Yet Luther was also able to speak about his trials and moments of despair as the work of the devil or of that dreadful coalition, "the world, the flesh and the devil."[40] The very things that are God's instruments to

---

36. *Commentary on Psalm 51:7* (1538) WA XL-II, 395.27-31 = LW 12, 358. *Commentary on Genesis 22:1, 2* (1538) WA XLIII, 203.23-24 = LW 4, 94-95.

37. H. Beintker, *Die Überwindung der Anfechtung bei Martin Luther: Eine Studie zu seiner Theologie nach den Operationes in Psalmos 1519-21* (Berlin: Evangelische, 1954), pp. 38-56 passim.

38. Bühler, *Die Anfechtung,* p. 7.

39. A. McGrath, *Luther's Theology of the Cross: Martin Luther's Theological Breakthrough* (Oxford: Blackwell; New Haven: Yale, 1985 [German original 1982]), pp. 170-71.

40. *Treatise on the New Testament* (1520) WA VI, 373.13 = LW 35, 105.

strengthen faith are weapons in the hand of Satan to destroy it.[41] In the great Galatians Commentary of 1535 Luther wrote:

> In affliction and in the conflict of conscience it is the devil's habit to frighten us with the Law and to set against us the consciousness of sin, our wicked past, the wrath and judgment of God, hell and eternal death, so that thus he may drive us into despair and pluck us from Christ.[42]

It is particularly through the power of that heinous lie — that God is not gracious, that there is no mercy or forgiveness available, that only strict justice will prevail and so you are irretrievably lost — that the devil seeks to gain his victory. His great ally in this is the Law of God itself, which stands against us with demands we have not and cannot meet as we should. Luther's response is repeated often throughout his teaching career, perhaps nowhere more eloquently than in the Galatians commentary:

> When the devil accuses us and says: "You are a sinner; therefore you are damned." "No," I say, "for I take refuge in Christ, who has given Himself for my sins. Therefore Satan, you will not prevail against me as you try to frighten me by showing me the magnitude of my sins and to plunge me into anguish, loss of faith, despair, hatred, contempt of God, and blasphemy. In fact, when you say that I am a sinner, you provide me with the armor and weapons against yourself, so that I may slit your throat with your own sword and trample you underfoot. You yourself are preaching the glory of God to me; for you are reminding me, a miserable and condemned sinner, of the fatherly love of God, who "so loved the world that He gave His only Son, etc." You are reminding me of the blessing of Christ my Redeemer. On his shoulders, not on mine, lie all my sins.[43]

The trial is real. The despair it may cause should never be dismissed as illusory or simply a quirk of the personality. Yet there is a lie close to the heart of the experience that must not be believed. God has not turned his back on those who trust him, even when that trust is faltering. We have a prom-

---

41. D. P. Scaer, "The Concept of *Anfechtung* in Luther's Thought," *Concordia Theological Quarterly* 47 (1983): 17.

42. *Commentary on the Argument of the Epistle to the Galatians* (1535) WA XL-I, 50.12-16 = LW 26, 10-11.

43. *Commentary on Galatians 1:4* (1535) WA XL-I, 89.19-90.10 = LW 26, 36-37.

ise to hold on to in the darkness. Characteristically, Luther would invoke the promise of God in baptism at this point.

> For this reason we must boldly and without fear hold fast to our baptism, and set it high against all sins and terrors of conscience. We must humbly admit, "I know full well that I cannot do a single thing that is pure. But I am baptized, and through my baptism God, who cannot lie, has bound himself in a covenant with me. He will not count my sin against me, but will slay it and blot it out.[44]

As one modern writer puts it, "right here in this horrible *Anfechtung,* where Satan is seeking to bring the Christian to the point of hating God, God is saving the sinner."[45]

Despair and the Theologian

Luther understood the struggle with despair as part and parcel of the Christian life. He did not minimize its seriousness; he did not explain it away or seek an easy remedy. He expected the struggle to continue even when the promises of God in Jesus Christ have been heard and believed. They are part of following Christ under the conditions of brokenness that will continue until he returns. Of course they are not the whole story. There is more to life as a follower of Jesus now than the *Anfechtungen.* There is plenty of scope for joy and thanksgiving and delight in the good things of creation. Luther took time to sniff a flower in the midst of his intense debate with the Catholic theologian Johann Eck. He delighted in his marriage to his Katie and spoke frequently about how wonderful it was to play with the children. But he insisted that a realistic assessment of life is called for if we are not to be wrong-footed by the devil when suffering inevitably comes.

Yet for Luther there was a particular benefit of these trials that he came to appreciate in the light of the gospel and his own role in its recovery. In the midst of the indulgence controversy in 1520 he summed it up in one of the most famous of his sayings: "It is not understanding, reading or speculation, but living, no dying and being damned that make a theologian."[46]

---

44. *The Holy and Blessed Sacrament of Baptism* (1519) WA II, 732.19-24 = LW 35, 36.
45. Scaer, "The Concept of *Anfechtung*," p. 25.
46. *Second Series of Psalms Lectures* (1519-21), WA V, 163.28-29.

Throughout his life Luther detested the kind of speculative theology that had dominated the universities of his age. He nailed his colors to the mast on this issue very early in his career as a Reformer. In the theses he prepared for the triennial meeting of his order in Heidelberg in 1518, he insisted

19. That person does not deserve to be called a theologian who looks upon the invisible things of God as though they were clearly perceptible in those things that have actually happened.
20. He deserves to be called a theologian, however, who comprehends the visible and manifest things of God seen through suffering and the cross.
21. A theology of glory calls evil good and good evil. A theology of the cross calls the thing what it actually is.[47]

For Luther theology, the knowledge of God, was an entirely practical matter. Of course it involved the intellect. Knowing God and speaking about him truthfully is served by careful study of the Bible and deep reflection on the God who reveals himself in this his word.[48] Yet for Luther knowing God was deeply experiential; it cut to the very heart of life. It orders priorities and reorients perspectives on the world and all it has to offer. Knowing God is not an idle academic exercise. When that *is* the case it is not God but some figment of your imagination you are talking about. The living God cannot be domesticated or quarantined and so in a very literal sense knowing God is dangerous. Every other prop will need to give way before him.

Luther came to see that the struggle with despair and hope is the proper context in which real theology, the genuine article, is done. As he would say at table in 1532, "experience alone makes a theologian."[49] Luther teased this out in a reflection on Psalm 119 that formed part of the preface to the Wittenberg edition of his German writings in 1539. There he found three critical elements for what he called "the correct way of studying theology" in contrast to the method advocated by his own teachers: prayer, meditation, and temptation. As we might expect, his accent is very definitely on the third.

---

47. *Heidelberg Disputation* (1518) WA I, 354.17-22 = LW 31, 40.

48. Luther had no difficulty in speaking about the Bible as the word of God without qualification, even if at other times he made clear that only Jesus Christ is the word of God in the sense of being divine (i.e., *substantialiter*). See Thompson, *A Sure Ground*, pp. 68-90.

49. #46 (1531) WATr I, 16.13 = LW 54, 7. See also above, n. 28.

Thirdly there is temptation, *Anfechtung*. This is the touchstone that teaches you not only to know and understand but also to experience how right and true, how sweet and lovely, how powerful and comforting God's word is, wisdom above all wisdom.[50]

The struggle with hopelessness, passing through those dark periods of despair, brings to light what is most valuable and most true in Christian theology. It unmasks the banality and superficiality of so much that goes by that name and forcibly draws our attention to our only hope, Christ himself. Theology tempered in this fire not only endures, it nourishes the faith of Christians in the meantime. It provides a context in which the Christian soul lays hold of God's precious promise, his word, and from that word receives real and lasting comfort.[51] Paradoxically, then, the devil arms his own enemies, the faithful theologians of God's word: "For as soon as God's Word takes root and grows in you, the devil will harry you, and will make a real doctor of you, and by his assaults will teach you to seek and love God's Word."[52] Luther told his students that this is exactly what had happened to him.

> I did not learn my theology all at once, but had to search constantly deeper and deeper for it. My temptations did that for me, for no one can understand Holy Scripture without practice and temptations. This is what the enthusiasts and sects lack. They don't have the right critic, the devil, who is the best teacher of theology. [. . .] If we don't have that kind of devil, then we become nothing but speculative theologians, who do nothing but walk around in our own thoughts and speculate with our reason alone as to whether things should be like this, or like that.[53]

What makes the difference then between idle speculation and true theology, at least in Luther's mind, is the urgency and single-mindedness that true theology gains from being forged in the furnace of struggle and de-

---

50. Preface to the Wittenberg Edition of the German Writings (1539) *WA* L, 660.1-4 = *LW* 34, 286-87.

51. *Adventspostille* (1522) *WA* X-I/2, 75.1-10.

52. Preface to the Wittenberg Edition of the German Writings (1539) *WA* L, 660.8-9 = *LW* 34, 287.

53. #352 (Autumn 1532) *WATr* I, 147.3-14 = *LW* 54, 50. Translation from Kleinig, "Oratio, Meditatio, Tentatio," pp. 256-57.

spair. And that is why he is able to say so shockingly that the devil is the best teacher of theology.

Despair Itself Brought Low

Already the lines of Luther's pastoral response to the dire reality of the struggle with despair have begun to emerge. "In the midst of the devil's teeth the Christian should keep to the word of grace." The true theologian is taught by his or her trials "to seek and love God's Word." It is remarkable how often a reference to the promises of Scripture is made in the context of Luther's discussions of the *Anfechtungen*. Even way back at the beginning, when he was still a monk in Erfurt, his father confessor had made the same connection, responding to his struggles by arranging for him to spend long hours in the memorization of Scripture. None of this was accidental. In fact it reflects what was consistently one of Luther's most basic theological commitments. In the manifesto on Christian liberty in 1520 he had made it clear: "The soul can do without anything except the word of God."[54] At Worms he had declared it for all to hear: "Here I stand. I cannot do otherwise. God help me. Amen." No wonder Luther would later advise, "We should not allow this staff of the promise to be wrested from our hands."[55] With such a promise there was light at the end of the tunnel of despair. "I will never leave you nor forsake you" (Heb. 13:5). "And behold I am with you always, to the end of the age" (Matt. 28:20). "Whoever believes in me, though he die, yet shall he live, and everyone who lives and believes in me shall never die" (John 11:25-26). "Whoever comes to me I will never cast out" (John 6:37).

The struggle with despair, Luther realized, is the struggle of the moment. It is a significant part of the shape of life between Jesus' resurrection and return. Triumphalism is a dangerous illusion that does not take seriously enough the simple fact that the world remains fractured and God's Christ is the crucified one. In this way Christian theology provides the resources to explain the larger context of each individual struggle with despair, and not only when that struggle has a conscious spiritual dimension. Despair is in fact part of universal human experience, for we all share in the brokenness, the frustration, and the groaning of the world awaiting its

54. *The Freedom of a Christian* (1520) WA VII, 22.9-10 = LW 31, 345.
55. *Commentary on Genesis* 22:1, 2 (1538) WA XLIII, 203.19-22 = LW 4, 94.

redemption (Rom. 8:20-21). The sense of being hemmed in, of there being no way out, of all hope and joy being drained from our lives must not be trivialized or dismissed as a tragic anomaly.

Luther knew, as did the apostle Peter, we are apt to be brought low by the false accusations not only of our own consciences, but of the malevolent enemy of humankind, the devil. He "prowls around," Peter wrote, "like a roaring lion seeking someone to devour" (1 Pet. 5:8). Like the other powers he was soundly defeated by the death and resurrection of Jesus, but he continues to peddle his lies with the dream that in the midst of despair some might abandon faith and hope. We have seen Luther's strategy for dealing with such assaults. He had a word for the accuser. Against his lies Luther would hold up the sure promise of God in the Scriptures. "No one can snatch me out of his hand," echoing the words of Jesus in John 10:28-29. "It is finished," the words proclaimed from the cross. Or simply, but pregnant with meaning, "I am baptized."

God can be trusted in the midst of the darkness and he has promised that the darkness will end. In the meantime the darkness strangely serves to keep us from so entangling ourselves in the present that we forget about hope. For a day is coming when the circumstances that drive us to despair, those we have engineered and those beyond our power to control, the restriction of our freedom and the oppressive opening up of a plethora of freedoms, will all finally be resolved. A day is coming when fear will be done away with and weeping will be a thing of the past. Our losses will be swallowed up by grace, and the guarantee is the cross of Christ. Hope can withstand the batterings of conscience and the false accusations of the evil one because Jesus died and rose again. Peace can anchor the tormented soul because Jesus died and rose again. Our failures have been dealt with and new life has begun.

Martin Luther was a man who knew despair from the inside and knew it in a remarkably intense way. He did not try to explain it away or dress it up or pretend it wasn't real. Yet he realized that true theology, a proper understanding of God and his purposes, provides the only genuine and effective counter to despair. The living God is not the impersonal executor of cosmic justice. Rather, the intensity of his involvement with us in the midst of our selfishness and perversity is seen in the gift of his Son.

Among all the other things that Luther did during his lifetime, he wrote hymns, grand hymns suffused with the rich theology he had learned in the midst of his *Anfechtungen*. Perhaps the best known is "A Mighty

Fortress Is Our God," written in 1527. The third verse rehearses again the hope that sustains in the midst of trials, temptations, and despair.

> And though this world with devils filled
> Should threaten to undo us
> We will not fear for God has willed
> His truth to triumph through us.
> The prince of darkness grim? We tremble not for him.
> His rage we can endure, for lo! His doom is sure.
> One little Word shall fell him.[56]

As James Kittelson once so memorably put it, "The 'little Word' was Christ."[57]

Abbreviations

LW   *Luther's Works,* edited by Jaroslav Pelikan and Helmut T. Lehmann. 55 vols. St. Louis/Philadelphia: Concordia/Fortress, 1955-86.

WA   *D. Martin Luthers Werke: Kritische Gesamtausgabe, Schriften,* edited by J. K. F. Knaake, G. Kawerau, et al. 71 vols. Weimar: Hermann Böhlaus Nachfolger, 1883-2004.

WABr   *D. Martin Luthers Werke: Kritische Gesamtausgabe, Briefwechsel,* edited by J. K. F. Knaafe, G. Kawerau, et al. 18 vols. Weimar: Hermann Böhlaus Nachfolger, 1930-85.

WATr   *D. Martin Luthers Werke: Kritische Gesamtausgabe, Tischreden,* edited by J. K. F. Knaake, G. Kawerau, et al. 6 vols. Weimar: Hermann Böhlaus Nachfolger, 1912-21.

Bibliography

Appel, H. *Anfechtung und Trost im Spätmittelalter und bei Luther.* Leipzig: Heinsius, 1938.

Beintker, H. *Die Überwindung der Anfechtung bei Martin Luther: Eine Studie zu*

---

56. The translation is that of Frederick H. Hedge.

57. J. M. Kittelson, *Luther the Reformer: The Story of the Man and His Career* (Leicester: InterVarsity Press, 1989 [American edition 1986]), p. 212.

seiner Theologie nach den Operationes in Psalmos 1519-21. Berlin: Evangelische, 1954.

Brecht, M. *Martin Luther: His Road to Reformation 1483-1521.* Translated by James L. Schaaf. German original 1981. Minneapolis: Fortress, 1985.

Brecht, M. *Martin Luther: Shaping and Defining the Reformation 1521-1532.* Translated by James L. Schaaf. German original 1986. Minneapolis: Fortress, 1990.

Brecht, M. *Martin Luther: The Preservation of the Church 1532-1546.* Translated by James L. Schaaf. German original 1987. Minneapolis: Fortress, 1993.

Bühler, P. T. *Die Anfechtung bei Martin Luther.* Zurich: Zwingli-Verlag, 1942.

Courtenay, W. J. "Between Despair and Love: Some Late Medieval Modifications of Augustine's Teaching on Fruition and Psychic States," pp. 5-19 in *Augustine, the Harvest, and Theology 1300-1650: Essays Dedicated to Heiko Augustinus Oberman in Honor of His Sixtieth Birthday,* edited by Kenneth Hagen. Leiden: Brill, 1990.

Dress, W. "Gerson und Luther," *Zeitschrift für Kirchengeschichte* 52 (1933): 122-61.

Durkheim, E. *Suicide: A Study in Sociology,* translated by John A. Spaulding and George Simpson. French original edition of 1930. Glencoe, Ill.: Free Press, 1951.

Erikson, E. H. *Young Man Luther: A Study in Psychoanalysis and History.* London: Faber and Faber, 1958.

Hovland, C. W. "Anfechtung in Luther's Biblical Exegesis," in *Reformation Studies: Essays in Honor of Roland H. Bainton,* edited by Franklin H. Littell. Richmond: John Knox, 1962, pp. 46-60.

Jüngel, E. *Anfechtung und Gewißheit des Glaubens oder wie die Kirche wieder zu ihrer Sache kommt.* München: Kaiser, 1976.

Kittelson, J. M. *Luther the Reformer: The Story of the Man and His Career.* American edition 1986. Leicester: IVP, 1989.

Klaas, W. *Anfechtung und Trost: Auslegungen ausgewählter Psalmen.* Neukirchen: Neukirchener, 1963.

Kleinig, J. W. "Oratio, Meditatio, Tentatio: What Makes a Theologian?," *Concordia Theological Quarterly* 66, no. 3 (2002): 255-67.

Lienhard, M. *Luther: Witness to Jesus Christ — Stages and Themes of the Reformer's Christology.* Translated by Edwin H. Robertson. French original 1973. Minneapolis: Augsburg, 1982.

Loewenich, W. von. *Martin Luther: The Man and His Work.* Translated by Lawrence W. Denef. German original 1982. Minneapolis: Augsburg, 1986.

McGrath, A. E. *Luther's Theology of the Cross: Martin Luther's Theological Breakthrough.* Oxford: Blackwell. German original 1982. New Haven: Yale, 1985.

Oberman, H. A. *Luther: Man Between God and the Devil.* Translated by Eileen Walliser-Schwarzbart. German original 1982. New Haven: Yale University Press, 1989.

Orcutt, J. D. *Analyzing Deviance.* Homewood, Ill.: Dorsey, 1983.

Ozment, S. E. *The Reformation in the Cities: The Appeal of Protestantism to Sixteenth-Century Germany and Switzerland.* New Haven: Yale University Press, 1975.

Rohr, J. von. "Medieval Consolation and the Young Luther's Despair," in *Reformation Studies: Essays in Honor of Roland H. Bainton,* edited by Franklin H. Littell. Richmond: John Knox, 1962, pp. 61-74.

Scaer, D. P. "The Concept of *Anfechtung* in Luther's Thought," *Concordia Theological Quarterly* 47 (1983): 15-30.

Schumann, F. K. *Gottesglaube und Anfechtung bei Luther.* Leipzig: Deichert, 1938.

Stendahl, K. "The Apostle Paul and the Introspective Conscience of the West," *Harvard Theological Review* 56, no. 3 (1963): 199-215.

Strohl, J. E. "Luther's Spiritual Journey," in *The Cambridge Companion to Martin Luther,* edited by Donald K. McKim. Cambridge: Cambridge University Press, 2003, pp. 149-64.

Thielicke, H. *Theologie der Anfechtung.* Tübingen: Mohr, 1949.

Thompson, M. D. *A Sure Ground on Which to Stand: The Relation Between Authority and Interpretive Method in Luther's Approach to Scripture.* Carlisle: Paternoster, 2002.

KIERKEGAARD
on Anxiety

PETER G. BOLT

*The creation waits with eager longing for the revealing of
the sons of God.*

(Romans 8:19)

Apparently the nineteenth-century Danish Christian philosopher Søren
Kierkegaard (1813-1855) was the first philosopher to recognize that many
people in our modern age experience feelings of "anxiety" for reasons not
easy to comprehend.

Although there are problems with attempting to define or describe
emotional states too narrowly, perhaps as a starting point we could say that
"Anxiety is that feeling of apprehension and dread that comes with the
perception that something bad might happen."[1]

Some would even say that we are currently living in an age of anxiety.

---

1. S. Edelman, *Change Your Thinking* (Sydney: ABC Books, 2002), p. 102. The standard
diagnostic manual for psychological conditions, DSM IV, does not attempt to define anxiety,
but simply classifies the various anxiety disorders on the basis of their symptoms.

1. The Age of Anxiety

1.1 Twenty-First-Century Australia

As the twenty-first century begins, to cite a case study from the Western world, many Australians are living with a level of anxiety that is severe enough to be regarded as a disorder.

In 1999 the federal government made an official announcement that depression was "the Ailment of the twenty-first century."[2] This led to some much-needed initiatives to help those suffering from this crippling illness. However, the 1997 report that lay behind this announcement, *Mental Health and Well-Being Profile of Adult Australians,* also revealed another problem that has not received as much publicity. Whereas in the previous twelve months 5.1 percent of Australians suffered from depression, 9.7 percent suffered from some kind of anxiety disorder.[3] Such figures suggest that in Australia, the twenty-first century could certainly be termed an age of anxiety.

But how unique is our twenty-first-century anxiety? It is interesting to notice that there have been many periods of human history that have also received the label "age of anxiety," from the twentieth century right back to the first-century Greco-Roman world.

1.2 First-Century Greco-Roman World

Once the term was coined by W. H. Auden,[4] the twentieth century was regularly described as an age of anxiety.[5] The label has been applied to the

---

2. *Mental Health: A Report Focussing on Depression,* http://www.health.gov.au/internet/wcms/publishing.nsf/content/health-mediarel-yr1999- mw-hmc5.htm (5 May 2006).

3. http://www.health.gov.au/internet/wcms/publishing.nsf/Content/health-archivemed iare1-1998-mw4398.htm (5 May 2006). Dr. Kathleen Griffiths, Director and Associate Professor of the Depression and Anxiety Consumer Research Unit, Canberra, confirmed that this report represents the latest research into Anxiety in Australia (per e-mail 8 May 2006).

4. E. R. Dodds, *Pagan and Christian in an Age of Anxiety: Some Aspects of Religious Experience from Marcus Aurelius to Constantine* (Cambridge: Cambridge University Press, 1965), p. 3.

5. R. Gerzon, *Finding Serenity in the Age of Anxiety* (New York: Macmillan, 1997); M. S. Peck, *The Road Less Traveled and Beyond: Spiritual Growth in an Age of Anxiety* (London: Rider, 1997); D. Rossinow, *The Politics of Authenticity: Liberalism, Christianity, and the New Left in America* (New York: Columbia University Press, 1998); A. J. Zuckermann, "Judaism and the Age of Anxiety," in S. A. Burrell, ed., *The Role of Religion in Modern European History* (New York: Macmillan, 1964).

post–World War II period[6] and to the post–World War I period.[7] But it has also been applied to earlier periods: early modern culture,[8] early seventeenth-century England,[9] and the medieval period[10] have all been described as ages of anxiety.

But we need to go even further back, to the period of late antiquity from Marcus Aurelius to the Christian Emperor Constantine. According to E. R. Dodds, this time in which the *Pax Romana* was slowly disintegrating was also an age of anxiety.[11] Dodds admitted that the limits of this period ought to be treated with "some elasticity."[12] If he had more space, he could easily have begun his inquiry with the age of Philo and St Paul![13] In other words, the first-century world could also be characterized as an age of anxiety. It, too, labored under great anxiety caused by events in the material world,[14] the dark forces of the demonic,[15] and the oppressive forces of the divine.[16]

And, of course, there is nothing new under the sun. Human beings'

6. American cultural analyst Arthur Schlesinger, Jr. spoke of the post–World War II period in these terms; see Rossinow, *Politics,* p. 3. Others have spoken of "atomic anxiety"; N. R. McRillis, "Atomic Anxiety in Cold War Britain: Science, Sin, and Uncertainty in Nuclear Monster Films," in George Aichele and Richard Walsh, eds., *Screening Scripture: Intertextual Connections Between Scripture and Film* (Harrisburg, Pa.: Trinity Press International, 2002).

7. Zuckerman, "Judaism," p. 133.

8. A. J. Bouwsma, "The Durable Renaissance: Anxiety and the Formation of Early Modern Culture," in William J. Bouwsma, *A Usable Past: Essays in European Cultural History* (Berkeley : University of California Press, 1990).

9. M. MacDonald, *Mystical Bedlam: Madness, Anxiety and Healing in Seventeenth-Century England* (Cambridge: Cambridge University Press, 1983). MacDonald examines the 2000-odd cases of Richard Napier in the years 1597-1634.

10. This anxiety has been connected with the rise of medieval mysticism: J. M. Nuth, *God's Lovers in an Age of Anxiety: The Medieval English Mystics* (London: Darton, Longman & Todd, 2001); R. Rohr and J. B. Feister, *Hope Against Darkness: The Transforming Vision of Saint Francis in an Age of Anxiety* (Cincinnati: St. Anthony Messenger Press, 2001).

11. Dodds, *Pagan and Christian.*

12. Dodds, *Pagan and Christian,* p. 4.

13. Dodds, *Pagan and Christian,* p. 3.

14. See K. Wengst, *Pax Romana and the Peace of Jesus Christ,* trans. J. Bowden (London: SCM, 1987 [German: 1986]).

15. For these forces with respect to health and magic, see P. G. Bolt, *Jesus' Defeat of Death: Persuading Mark's Early Readers,* SNTSMS 125 (Cambridge: Cambridge University Press, 2003).

16. These were the topics of Dodds's first three lectures, now printed in *Pagan and Christian.* The fourth dealt with the dialogue between paganism and Christianity.

sense of anxiety and alienation is as old as the Greek Tragedies; as old as the Epic of Gilgamesh, in which humanity is threatened with destruction for disturbing the slumber of the gods.[17] It is as old as Adam and Eve sewing together their fig leaves to cover the glory of their nakedness.

To be human in this fallen world is to be anxious. Human beings have always lived in an age of anxiety. But the first-century Greco-Roman world was different from other times in one significant respect. For into that anxious context, a new group known as "Christians" began to seriously answer the anxiety of every age. And, before long, their movement spread across the first-century world like a tidal wave.

1.3 When the time was fulfilled . . .

When Jesus began his ministry, he spoke as if things were about to change dramatically: "The time is fulfilled, and the kingdom of God is at hand" (Mark 1:15).

This was a message that made promises on the grandest scale. The entire sweep of human history was brought together as pointing to exactly this moment of fulfillment. The future of the world was now focused on a single event with equally grand consequences: the kingdom of God had drawn near.

Jesus makes no explicit mention of the anxiety of the age he had now entered. How does the age of the Messiah, with the promise of the age to come, affect our understanding of the age of anxiety in which we continue to live? More importantly, does the message of Jesus bring us any consolation to our anxious lives, and if so, how? And if this consolation exists, how does Søren Kierkegaard help us to think about it further?

2. Anxiety and the Gospel?

2.1 Simple Instructions

The first thing to notice is that the Bible apparently says very little about anxiety. The NT has two well-known verses giving us some instruction:

17. Zuckerman, "Judaism," p. 135.

Philippians 4:6 — Do not be anxious about anything, but in everything by prayer and supplication with thanksgiving let your requests be made known to God.

1 Peter 5:6-7 — Humble yourselves, therefore, under the mighty hand of God so that at the proper time he may exalt you, casting all your anxieties on him, because he cares for you.

These are simple, and straight to the point. They address anxiety and tell Christian people to get rid of it. Now, it must be said that at first glance this kind of approach seems rather simplistic. But, before damning these verses too quickly, we should hold off until the end of our inquiry. For, given the practice discerned elsewhere in the NT when it deals with commands or prohibitions, it is highly likely that these counsels to remove anxiety represent the tip of an iceberg. If this is so, we may find that underneath these simple instructions there lies a profound understanding of God, the world, and ourselves, that promises the most significant medicine for the anxious soul that could possibly be administered.

Strictly speaking, there is only one main word-family in the NT that conveys the sense of the feeling we describe as "anxiety," that is, the family μεριμνάω, μέριμνα, which is used in three distinct settings.[18] A survey of these usages will set the parameters for our more profound response to anxiety in company with Kierkegaard.

By far the majority of usages of this word in the NT are in the context of anxiety about the things of this world.

2.2 *The Anxiety of Insecurity*

2.2.1 *The Worries of an Insecure World*

a) Worry About the Ordinary Things of This Life   Jesus warned his hearers about the worries of this life that afflict human beings on a daily basis.

Matthew 6:25 (cf. Luke 12:22) — Therefore I tell you, do not worry about your life, what you will eat or drink; or about your body, what you will wear. Is not life more important than food, and the body more important than clothes?

18. These three usages are reflected in the headings to follow.

Matthew 6:27 (cf. Luke 12:25-26) — Who of you by worrying can add a single hour to his life?

Matthew 6:28 — And why do you worry about clothes? See how the lilies of the field grow. They do not labor or spin.

Matthew 6:31 — So do not worry, saying, "What shall we eat?" or "What shall we drink?" or "What shall we wear?"

Matthew 6:34 — Therefore do not worry about tomorrow, for tomorrow will worry about itself. Each day has enough trouble of its own.

In Luke's account of the two sisters, Martha and Mary, Martha is presented as an example of someone who is caught up in such concerns: "Martha, Martha," the Lord answered, "you are worried and troubled about many things, [. . .]" (Luke 10:41). But it is important to realize that this is simply normal in a world like ours. There is a profound insecurity at the heart of our world. This racing around after what to eat, drink, and wear is part of what we feel is necessary to survive. Such anxiety is a daily reminder that we live under the shadow of the grave (cf. Heb. 2:14-15).

b) Worry About the Ordinary Relationships of This Life   And, of course, the anxieties of ordinary life are escalated by the fact that we are not simply individuals. We are husbands, wives, parents, children. We live in families, as part of a wider tribe. We have friends, relatives, neighbors. Our relational networks bring us all kinds of extra anxiety. This, too, is just part of ordinary life. To take this relational responsibility seriously brings its own anxiety.

Think of Paul's instructions about marriage and singleness, for example.

1 Corinthians 7:32 — I would like you to be free from anxiety. An unmarried man is anxious about the Lord's affairs — how he can please the Lord;

1 Corinthians 7:33 — but a married man is anxious about the affairs of this world — how he can please his wife,

1 Corinthians 7:34 — and his interests are divided. An unmarried woman or virgin is anxious about the Lord's affairs: Her aim is to be devoted to the Lord in both body and spirit. But a married woman is anxious about the affairs of this world — how she can please her husband.

c) Worry About the Extraordinary Threats to This Life   In such an insecure world, where we are anxious daily about whether and how we, and
our loved ones, are going to survive, there is always the additional possibility of extraordinary threats to life. The whole series of apocalyptic woes
have always been and will always be a part of the fabric of this fallen world.
There will be famines and plagues; wars and rumors of wars; nation will
rise against nation; kingdom will rise against kingdom (cf. Mark 13:7-8).
This cosmic upheaval forms the general backdrop of our ordinary existence, raising anxiety about a whole variety of extraordinary threats to life
as we know it. In such a world, in which those who are called Benefactors
among us lord it over their subjects (cf. Luke 22:25), Jesus' followers could
be dragged before the politico-legal powers. But, he said, "When they arrest you, do not worry about what to say or how to say it" (Matt. 10:19;
Luke 12:11; cf. Mark 13:9-11).

If this world is such an insecure place, why did Jesus warn against the
anxiety that seems to be simply a part of our ordinary existence? There is a
great danger lurking here: the anxieties of this insecure world can lead
people away from the living God.

2.2.2 *The Danger of Such Worldly Anxiety*

In Jesus' famous "Parable of the Sower," among the four types of soil, the
third, the thorny ground, reveals a very ordinary kind of danger:

> Still others, like seeds sown among thorns, hear the word; but the wor-
> ries of this life, the deceitfulness of wealth and the desires for other
> things come in and choke the word, making it unfruitful. (Mark 4:18-19;
> cf. Matt. 13:22 and Luke 8:14)

Martha provides an illustration of someone caught up in the worries of
this life (Luke 10:41). Jesus also spoke of his contemporaries among the
people of Israel as those who were caught up in such worries. Instead of
being ready for the Son of Man when he arrived, they were like those in the
days of Noah, or those in the days of Lot, "eating, drinking, marrying and
being given in marriage, [. . .] buying and selling, planting and building"
(Luke 17:27-28), being so caught up with ordinary life that they missed the
dramatic moment in which they were standing. Jesus looked ahead to his
own installation as the glorious Son of Man, and warned his contemporar-

ies: "Be careful, or your hearts will be weighed down with dissipation, drunkenness and the anxieties of life, and that day will close on you unexpectedly like a trap" (Luke 21:34).

The anxiety that is so much a part of this insecure world is dangerous. It so distracts human beings that they miss out on seeing the most important thing in all of human history. They can hear the word that the Messiah has come, but the anxieties of life strangle that message.

That is the first way this word is used in the NT, to speak of the anxiety aroused by our insecure existence in this fallen world.

2.3 The Call to Pray Rather Than Being Anxious

More briefly, the second context in which the anxiety words are used is that of a call to pray, in the midst of our anxiety. Here we return to our two famous texts:

> Philippians 4:6 — Do not be anxious about anything, but in everything by prayer and supplication with thanksgiving let your requests be made known to God.
> 1 Peter 5:6-7 — Humble yourselves, therefore, under the mighty hand of God so that at the proper time he may exalt you, casting all your anxieties on him, because he cares for you.

Prayer is the practical response to anxiety. Prayer, of course, comes within the larger context of remembering the lesson of the lily and the bird, that we have a Heavenly Father who cares for us (Matt. 6:26-30). Prayer also comes within the larger context of seeking first God's kingdom and his righteousness (Matt. 6:33). As we live in this insecure world, with the anxiety aroused by ordinary life and ordinary relationships, as well as the constant possibility of extraordinary threats to life, the gospel tells us that there is another, more important reality to remember. Jesus Christ has come, and by his life, death, and resurrection, he has brought us the way to the powerful God who *will* establish his kingdom. Jesus Christ has brought us to the heavenly Father who cares, and who invites us to pray to him in the midst of our anxiety.

Rather surprisingly, once this gospel perspective is grasped, a revolution takes place in human life. Instead of the usual anxiety about my own life, with all of its narrowing and constricting effects, Jesus Christ introduces a new kind of anxiety, a positive anxiety for God, and for his people.

2.4 Positive Anxiety for God and His People

2.4.1 Anxiety for the Things of the Lord

Instead of worrying about the ordinary necessities of this life, Jesus told his followers that this was our Heavenly Father's department. Instead, seek first his kingdom and righteousness, and all these things will be added. If his disciples had to face up to political forces, they would be supplied with the right words to say. God is the one in charge: he is the one who will speak through them. Remember, too, Paul's instructions about marriage and singleness, for example.

> 1 Corinthians 7:32 — I would like you to be free from anxiety. An unmarried man is anxious about the Lord's affairs — how he can please the Lord.
> 1 Corinthians 7:34 — An unmarried woman or virgin is anxious about the Lord's affairs: Her aim is to be devoted to the Lord in both body and spirit.

Here, of course, the basic thing the apostle commends is to be anxious about the things of the Lord. Whether unmarried or married, that should be what consumes our existence.

2.4.2 Anxiety for Christ's People

This involves such a transformation of life that the Christian person begins to be worried, not about themselves, but about others. This is exemplified in the apostolic ministry, when Paul could say: "Besides everything else, I face daily the pressure of my anxiety for all the churches" (2 Cor. 11:28). Or when he could speak of Timothy as being the only one who was genuinely anxious about the Philippians (Phil. 2:20).

But such positive anxiety is also meant to be a part of every congregation. The Corinthian church hadn't really got the message, even using their spiritual gifts to divide and conquer congregational life. But Paul puts them right by expounding the way of love (1 Cor. 13), and by reminding them that God has given honor to every member of the body of Christ, "so that there should be no division in the body, but that its members might be anxious equally for each other" (1 Cor. 12:25).

2.5 The Profound Gospel Promises

This survey of the three settings in which the NT vocabulary of anxiety is found, hints that the gospel has something profound to say to our anxious world. The NT usage begins with a pattern of anxiety in ordinary life, but moves towards viewing this anxiety in the context of a relationship with God, which then issues in a changed way of relating to other human beings. The anxious striving for survival, which characterizes the dog-eat-dog existence of our pagan and materialistic surroundings, is replaced by the other-person-centered harmony of the body of Christ.

The gospel promises form the substructure of the entire NT message. Against these promises, even the instructions to get rid of anxiety find their proper meaning. The gospel brings God's own solution to the world's problems, including the world's anxiety. There is nothing simplistic about God's promised solutions, for they address the profoundest levels of our existence. God promises ontological solutions, that is, solutions at the depths of our being, which then work outward to the rest of our lives. In Christ, God deals with who we are, and this changes how we live.

So how does God's solution address the problem of human anxiety? How can we think profoundly about this constant aspect of human life?

As we engage in this task, the nineteenth-century Danish thinker Søren Kierkegaard might be able to help us.

3. Introducing Søren Kierkegaard

3.1 His Influence

Søren Kierkegaard was born in 1813 and died in 1855. As has often been the case for great thinkers, Kierkegaard was largely criticized by his own contemporaries. On the other hand, his influence on *our* contemporaries has been enormous, even if indirectly, mediated through existentialist philosophers such as Karl Jaspers (1883-1969), Martin Heidegger (1889-1976),[19] Gabriel Marcel (1889-1973), Martin Buber (1878-1965), and Jean-Paul Sartre (1905-1980); psychologists such as (again) Karl Jaspers, Sigmund Freud (1856-1939), and Erich Fromm (1900-1980); Protestant theologians such as Karl Barth (1886-1968) and Paul Tillich (1886-1965); and post-modernists and deconstructionists such as Jacques Derrida (1930-2004).

In particular, Kierkegaard's conception of anxiety or dread *(Angst)* is now famous. Who hasn't heard or used the expression "existential Angst" — even if nobody really knows where it comes from, or even what it really means! The fame of this conception is partly due to its undeniable influence upon twentieth-century philosophers like Sartre and Heidegger, but also because it seems to ring true about certain states of mind that are recognizable at the level of ordinary human experience.[20]

Kierkegaard's enormous influence raises an interesting difficulty. Many of the recent thinkers influenced by him took his thought in different directions. He had a huge influence on secular existentialism, for example, yet whereas his project was an attempt to understand human experience from an avowedly Christian point of view, his secular followers consistently stripped his thought from its theological moorings.[21] By the same token, his influence on modern psychology can also be traced, but in this arena his thought has also been stripped of any reference to Christian theology. The challenge is therefore to read Kierkegaard on his own terms, rather than through the prism of the history of his influence. He was certainly someone who showed great insight into the human condition, being deeply touched by it himself, but he was not simply a humanist. As he reflected upon humanity, he did so as someone who had been just as profoundly touched by the grace of God in Jesus Christ. He was not simply interested in human beings; he was interested in human beings before the living God.

---

19. P. L. Gardiner, *Kierkegaard* (Oxford: Oxford University Press, 1988), p. 106. For further discussion of the relationship between the two philosophers, see D. Magurshak, "The Concept of Anxiety: A Keystone of the Kierkegaard — Heidegger Relationship," in R. L. Perkins, ed., *The International Kierkegaard Commentary: The Concept of Anxiety* (Macon, Ga.: Mercer University Press, 1985).

20. Despite the difficulty of some of Kierkegaard's discussions, his psychological works are studded with all kinds of stories and concrete examples that "frequently display a sharp percipience" (Gardiner, *Kierkegaard*, p. 110).

21. Cf. Gardiner, *Kierkegaard*, p. 108.

3.2. The Man[22]

To briefly summarize Kierkegaard, the man: He studied theology and philosophy, but he never took up a pastorate, giving his life to thinking and writing instead. Once he began writing, he entered what has been called a period of "furious scribbling," writing thirty-five books mostly in the eight years between 1842 and 1850, and filling twenty-two volumes of his journals — not to mention his letters, newspaper articles, dissertations, and a series of diatribes against clerics and magazine editors.

If Søren Kierkegaard lay upon a contemporary psychiatrist's couch, plenty of potential causes for anxiety would be exposed.

He was a frail child and he suffered from curvature of the spine, mysterious fits that left him weak, and an aversion to sunlight.

He did not have a good relationship with his father. Michael Kierkegaard was 56 when Søren was born. He had a rather dark and grim Christianity, and his child-rearing was rather authoritarian. His youngest son grew up admiring his father greatly, but also fearing him.

Søren and his brother Peter were the only two of seven children who survived the ravages of accident, disease, and childbirth complications. When Søren was 22, his father revealed a dreadful secret that he had harbored for most of his life. At the age of 11 Michael was minding his family's sheep out on the Jutland Moors. He was cold and hungry and the 11-year-old boy had cursed God. Michael confessed to Søren that he felt he had brought a curse upon the family, and God was punishing him by finishing off his children one by one. Peter and Søren accepted this explanation and became convinced that they, too, would die young.

Although he began studying to be a Lutheran pastor, Søren withdrew from university and left the family home to live the life of an "aesthete." Doubting his own Christian faith, he discovered literature, the opera, philosophy, drink, and girls, but the futility of such a life soon pressed in upon him, and he sank into despair at his lack of direction and his remoteness

22. For these and further biographical details, see D. Robinson and O. Zarate, *Introducing Kierkegaard* (Duxford, U.K.: Icon, 2003); Gardiner, *Kierkegaard*; J. Garff, *Søren Kierkegaard: A Biography*, trans. B. H. Kirmmse (Princeton and Oxford: Princeton University Press, 2005 [Danish: 2000]); A. Hannay, *Kierkegaard: A Biography* (Cambridge: Cambridge University Press, 2001); W. Lowrie, *Kierkegaard*, 2 vols. (Oxford: Oxford University Press, 1938; New York: Harper & Row, 1962); D. Palmer, *Kierkegaard for Beginners* (London: Writers and Readers Limited, 1996); M. Watts, *Kierkegaard* (Oxford: Oneworld, 2003).

from his friends. At the age of 25, his faith was rekindled and he was reconciled with his father, just three months before Michael died.

One of Kierkegaard's own prayers sums up his early days by saying: "O my God, my God, unhappy and tormented was my childhood, full of torments my youth. I have lamented, I have sighed, and I have wept."[23] It is important, however, not to interpret his ideas *expressively,* that is, as if he was always merely writing about himself. Certainly this has been a favorite game among his scholarly readers, but we should avoid this tendency.[24]

Of course his own personal difficulties influenced him, but they also provided the occasion for him to think profoundly, not only about his own life, but also about life in general and life before God. As such, reading Kierkegaard is less like reading his autobiography, and more like being profoundly engaged with our own. As the twentieth-century existentialist philosopher Jean-Paul Sartre put it: "Reading Kierkegaard, I climb back as far as myself. I want to catch hold of him, and it is myself I catch."[25]

3.3 The Book: The Concept of Anxiety (1844)

In 1844, Kierkegaard published his fifth major book, *Begrebet Angest,* under the pseudonym Vigilius Haufniensis, or "Watcher of the Marketplace."[26] This book is often cited as one of his most difficult to understand: "an intricate discussion";[27] "its positive content — perhaps inevitably in the context — remains elusive and finally mysterious."[28]

Exactly a century after its Danish publication, Walter Lowrie produced the first English translation under the title: *The Concept of Dread* (1944).[29] Almost forty years later, another English translation appeared, with the

23. P. D. LeFevre, ed., *The Prayers of Kierkegaard* (Chicago: University of Chicago Press, 1956), p. 77.

24. Gardiner, *Kierkegaard,* p. 110. Palmer, *Kierkegaard,* p. 26, states that Kierkegaard claimed no relation to his pseudonymous works, in particular, except as a reader.

25. From Palmer, *Kierkegaard,* p. 29.

26. In 1841 he published his M.A. dissertation, *The Concept of Irony;* in 1843 *Either/Or* and *Fear and Trembling;* and in 1844 *Philosophical Fragments* and *The Concept of Anxiety.* "Copenhagen" means marketplace in Danish.

27. Gardiner, *Kierkegaard,* p. 109.

28. Gardiner, *Kierkegaard,* p. 110.

29. *Kierkegaard's The Concept of Dread,* trans. W. Lowrie (Princeton: Princeton University Press, 1944).

English rendering of the title slightly changed to *The Concept of Anxiety* (1980).[30] Both translations also had a version of Kierkegaard's explanatory subtitle: in 1944: A *Simple Psychological Deliberation Oriented in the Direction of the Dogmatic Problem of Original Sin,* and in 1980: A *Simple Psychologically Orienting Deliberation on the Dogmatic Issue of Hereditary Sin.*

The subtitle explains why this book is referred to as one of his "psychological works."[31] We need to be aware, however, that Kierkegaard is using the word "psychology" in a different sense to what we might mean by the term today. After all, as a man of the early nineteenth century, he was writing well before the rise of modern psychology. In fact, he was one of its influences, through Freud and others. Kierkegaard's psychological discussion of anxiety is a discussion we might call *properly psychological.* He discusses anxiety as it relates to our *psyche,* our soul, our self, our very life and being.

For Kierkegaard, a human being is body-soul-spirit. The body gives us our physical relation to our world, the soul is our life-force. The synthesis of our body and soul is our spirit, and it is the destiny of man in the purposes of God that we should become spirit.[32] By becoming spirit we relate to our Creator, and so to his creation, properly. This is Kierkegaard's understanding of psychology, that is, of how a person is made up.

But notice, too, that he is also making a contribution toward theology, because, as the subtitle tells us, this book about anxiety is a psychologically oriented deliberation *on the dogmatic issue of Hereditary Sin.* How does "original sin" bear in upon our anxiety? How does our anxiety relate to Adam and what we have inherited from him?

4. An Anatomy of Anxiety

4.1 *What Is Anxiety?*

This Danish thinker distinguished "anxiety" (or "dread") from the ordinary fear that renders us some protection from harm. Once this is said, it is

---

30. *The Concept of Anxiety: A Simple Psychologically Orienting Deliberation on the Dogmatic Issue of Hereditary Sin,* ed. and trans. R. Thomte and A. B. Anderson (Princeton: Princeton University Press, 1980).

31. Gardiner, *Kierkegaard,* p. 103.

32. Martin, *Kierkegaard,* p. 82.

necessary to enter into his thought a little further in order to understand what his concept of anxiety is all about.

> There is no exact English equivalent for the Danish term *"Angst"* used by Kierkegaard. In general, it stands for that feeling of apprehension which arises in man as an agonizing premonition of evil, but which has no objective basis. It is a kind of horror at an undefined possibility; a fearful apprehension of the uncertain future; a terrifying presentiment of some unknown but possible peril.[33]

It is also important to notice that Kierkegaard is describing something that must be lived through at practically every moment of the day.[34]

Anxiety must be distinguished from fear, since this is common to animals and human beings. Anxiety is related to the fact that a human being is — or ought to be — qualified as "spirit."[35] Whereas fear arises from a real, concrete thing in the real world, anxiety is about nothing, that is, it arises from a mere possibility, something that is not actually the case, but is only potential.

Anxiety must also be distinguished from despair.[36] For Kierkegaard, in God's plan human beings must become spirit, or, to put it simply, they must will to become the person God wants them to be. A person is in despair when they give up on that project. They give up on becoming spirit, and so — whether consciously or unconsciously — they give up on becoming who they were created to be, and in so doing, they make a choice to become nothing.[37] Anxiety, on the other hand, arises from the very act of becoming spirit, of becoming who you were created to be. It arises from the possibility that exists in the actual experience of our freedom.

To illustrate: at the moment just prior to an act of will, I am aware of my freedom to choose. My freedom is real. It is actual. But as I am about to use my freedom to choose, I am aware of the various possibilities that exist before me. At this moment, the things I could choose are not *actual;* they

---

33. Martin, *Kierkegaard*, p. 83.

34. As opposed to Heidegger, for example. See G. Pattison, *Kierkegaard and the Crisis of Faith: An Introduction to His Thought* (London: SPCK, 1997), p. 102.

35. Martin, *Kierkegaard*, p. 83.

36. Pattison, *Kierkegaard*, p. 101.

37. Such a person wishes to become nothing, but "because he cannot consume himself, cannot get rid of himself, cannot become nothing." These ideas are explored in *The Sickness unto Death.*

are merely *possible*. This is why anxiety is not fear, which is related to something concrete, whereas anxiety is related to "something that is nothing."[38] Thus, I experience the actuality of my freedom, but this also alerts me to the possibility of various possibilities. This situation arouses anxiety, and here, anxiety is "freedom's actuality experienced as the possibility of possibility."[39]

This is, of course, a major aspect of Kierkegaard's discussion that was picked up and developed by the later existentialists. But there is more to say about his anatomy of anxiety than this. For, as the subtitle reveals, this book is not just an inquiry into some kind of autonomous freedom possessed by human beings, it is a psychological inquiry into the doctrine of hereditary sin. Our "existential Angst" needs to be understood against the backdrop of Adam's fall.

4.2 Hereditary Sin and Anxiety

Kierkegaard was unhappy with the explanations of hereditary sin that were current at the time.[40] He reacted against Hegel, who effectively denied the *fact* of original sin — since a necessary evolution is not sin. But he also found the explanation of Lutheran orthodoxy to be problematic, in which Adam's sin ended up being different from our own, effectively removing Adam from his connection with the race to follow him, and also from the benefits of Christ's atonement.

> The entire problem, then, is reduced to the search for some situation common to Adam and to us (so that he remains within the series), which at the same time allows us to explain a definitive change in mankind with the first sin.[41]

Kierkegaard's solution is found in his concept of anxiety. Anxiety connects Adam's first sin with all sins to follow. When the Lord told Adam not to eat of the tree of the knowledge of good and evil (Gen. 2:16-17), this

---

38. Kierkegaard, *Concept of Anxiety*, pp. 41-42.

39. Kierkegaard, *Concept of Anxiety*, p. 42.

40. L. Dupré, *Kierkegaard the Theologian: The Dialectic of Christian Existence* (New York: Sheed & Ward, 1963), pp. 50-51.

41. Dupré, *Kierkegaard*, p. 51.

awakened in Adam the sense of his own freedom. By being given the prohibition, he became aware that he was able to act either way, arousing in him anxiety — especially given the threat of death that had now become a possibility. He may not have known what it meant to be able, and he may not have known what it meant to die, but these possibilities were now presented to him as he became aware of the actuality of his freedom.[42] This was his state of anxiety prior to the action he took. And we know the end of the story.

Thus, to summarize Kierkegaard's view of the fall:

> Sin originates in a leap of freedom from innocence to guilt, under an awakened dread [=anxiety].[43]

Anxiety is therefore the middle term between innocence and guilt. Adam resolves his anxiety by making the wrong choice, and thus he becomes guilty of the first sin, leading to dreadful consequences for the world. Adam's sin introduces two kinds of anxiety.

> Anxiety as it appeared in Adam will never again return, for by him sinfulness came into the world. Because of this, Adam's anxiety has two analogies, the objective anxiety in nature and the subjective anxiety in the individual.[44]

4.3 Objective Anxiety

By Adam's sin, the world actually changed. As Paul put it, "by one man sin entered into the world, and through sin, death" (Rom. 5:12). Meditating upon this verse, Kierkegaard introduces the first kind of anxiety experienced by Adam's descendants:

> By coming into the world, sin acquired significance for the whole creation. This effect of sin in nonhuman existence I have called objective anxiety.[45]

42. Cf. Martin, *Kierkegaard*, p. 83.
43. Martin, *Kierkegaard*, p. 81.
44. Kierkegaard, *Concept of Anxiety*, p. 60.
45. Kierkegaard, *Concept of Anxiety*, p. 57.

He then calls attention to ἀποκαραδοκία τῆς κτίσεως, "the anxious long-ing of creation" (Rom. 8:19).

> This anxiety in creation may rightly be called objective anxiety. It is not brought forth by creation but by the fact that creation is placed in an entirely different light because of Adam's sin.[46]

Prior to his first sin, Adam did not experience this objective anxiety. This is one difference between him and his descendants.[47] There is no difference between Adam and the rest of us in terms of the *quality* of anxiety that precedes action, but there is a difference in terms of the *quantity* of anxiety. Because of Adam's sin, there is "a *quantitative increase* of dread."[48] Now the whole world is groaning in anxiety. There is a severe disturbance in all of creation, and we human beings are caught up in this objective anxiety. This means that there is a profound disturbance at the core of our being as we live as part of a world subjected to frustration.

At this point, Kierkegaard's objective anxiety is a psychological explanation of how our mortality works its negative power in our lives. Death came through sin, but the fact that we are mortal then leads to a state in which we are further prone to sin. As sinners, we now live under the shadow of death, and our mortal bodies have an objective anxiety, a core insecurity, built into them, that provides a drive toward sin. With the grave as our only future we live under a constant fear of death — and this is a deep, objective fear; it is present for all people, whether or not someone might consciously be aware of a fear of death at the surface-level.[49] This deep anxiety raised by our mortality brings us into slavery for our entire lives (Heb. 2:14-15). We seek to cope with this soul-level insecurity by following the desires of the flesh, by desperately seeking after security in this insecure world through material goods, or the pleasures of the moment ("eat, drink, and be merry"), or status, power, family connections, educa-

46. Kierkegaard, *Concept of Anxiety*, p. 58.

47. "The only point that differentiates Adam's sin from others, is that it brought sin *into a sinless* world. This qualitative change in the human condition [. . .] was immediately reflected in the universe; [. . .] a shadow fell upon the whole creation" (Dupré, *Kierkegaard*, p. 58).

48. Dupré, *Kierkegaard*, pp. 58-59.

49. We should note that although the Bible uses the word "fear," this verse nevertheless falls under the rubric of "anxiety" by the Kierkegaardian definition, because death for the individual is not an actuality, but a possibility.

tion, and all kinds of other idols that promise to deal with the objective anxiety that is built into our very bodies. But, of course, the security offered here is only for a season (cf. Heb. 11:25), and its promises are, in the end, ephemeral hopes that will eventually disappoint.

4.4 Subjective Anxiety

The second kind of anxiety in which we live in this fallen world, Kierkegaard labels "Subjective Anxiety." Once again, there is no *qualitative* difference between our experience and Adam's, but there is a *quantitative* difference. Prior to his first sin, Adam didn't experience objective anxiety, and so, in terms of objective anxiety, his experience was *less* than ours. After his sin, however, his descendants still experience subjective anxiety, but, in terms of *subjective* anxiety, Adam's experience was *more* than ours.

4.4.1 Subjective Anxiety and the Spirit

As the description suggests, subjective anxiety is experienced within the individual. This anxiety arises when a person has set before them the possibility of becoming spirit. This is the anxiety already described above, when the individual experiences his or her freedom, and this freedom raises various possibilities, and this arouses anxiety. Kierkegaard compares this anxiety to vertigo, or dizziness.

> Anxiety is the dizziness of freedom, which emerges when the spirit wants to posit the synthesis and freedom looks down into its own possibility.[50]

But, of course, Adam's situation before the fall is very different to our own. Adam's subjective anxiety was more than ours, because his freedom was more than ours. Once sin entered into the world, freedom is not experienced in the same sense as Adam's. Yet, despite the real differences in the situation, Adam's first sin is repeated in each of our sins as we follow in his footsteps.

---

50. Kierkegaard, *Concept of Anxiety,* p. 61. Cf. Pattison, *Kierkegaard,* p. 102.

4.4.2 The Moment

To help explain this similarity between our sin and Adam's first sin, we can turn to Kierkegaard's explanation of "the moment." It is possible to conceptualize every action as having a moment in which that action is willed, or decided. In this fallen world, this moment is when we decide to sin or not to sin. In this sense, the moment before we act, when sin is a real possibility, is qualitatively exactly the same as the moment before Adam's first sin. And, of course, this is the moment that is filled with anxiety as freedom's possibility is awakened.

Now this language of "the moment" is still used in contemporary psychology in dealing with anxious clients.[51] The strategy is to try to help the anxious person to live "in the moment." If anxiety is an over-concern about the possibilities that still lie in the future, it makes good sense to try to focus the mind upon the moment you are in and in which you must act right now.

Philosophically, the "moment" is an ancient conception, with roots in Plato. For Plato, "the moment" was between rest and motion. It is at this point Kierkegaard would offer an important correction both to Plato and to modern psychology.

For the "moment," for Kierkegaard, is not simply the present time that we are in right now, the time between rest and the next action. It is not simply a temporal conception, but it is a theological conception. Kierkegaard pointed out that even the aesthete, the pleasure seeker, lived for the present.[52] But Kierkegaard points out that in his pursuit of pleasure, the aesthete, to his great loss, fails to become "spirit." If the moment is viewed only temporally, it can be an incentive to sin. The choice to sin is a choice away from becoming spirit. In the end it is to choose death.

For Kierkegaard the moment must be viewed *theologically:* as I stand here in my freedom, about to act one way or the other, with all the anxiety that is therefore aroused, I must see myself in this moment as a being be-

---

51. See, for example, the suggested coping strategy, "I just need to take it slowly, one step at a time," (S. Edelman, *Change Your Thinking* [Sydney: ABC Books, 2002], p. 134), or the use of yoga, relaxation techniques, meditation, breathing exercises, which all help to "tune in" to the body right now (cf. pp. 128-32).

52. Contemporary psychiatry also recognizes the problems of being "caught in the present"; see R. Meares, *Intimacy and Alienation: Memory, Trauma and Personal Being* (London and Philadelphia: Routledge, 2000), p. 123.

fore God, who must act in such a way as to become "spirit," that is, I must choose to become the person that God wants me to be.

4.5 Necessary Anxiety

It is clear that, for Kierkegaard, this anxiety is necessary. It is what distinguishes us from animals, who do not have a destiny in the divine plan to become "spirit."

The existentialists drew upon Kierkegaard to say that the individual must feel the anxiety of the moment of decision, and by choosing to act, so they become human. This is true insofar as it goes, but, once again, we need to restore Kierkegaard's theological perspective. As we stand in the moment, we stand as a being before God, who must become spirit. As we feel the anxiety of our freedom's possibilities, we need to act in order to become the person that God wants us to be.

To put this in language more familiar to us from the New Testament, we need to act in the light of the future kingdom of God; in the light of our life, which is now hidden with Christ at the right hand of God (Col. 3:1-4). As we do so, we become truly human, as we are conformed more and more to the image of our Creator in his beloved Son.

Thus, anxiety is necessary to become fully human.

But there is another, more philosophical sense in which this anxiety is "necessary." In this fallen world we have come a long way from the freedom to act that Adam enjoyed in the Garden of Eden. In this world in which sin has now entered and become sinfulness, sin becomes more and more *possible* to one's freedom. As we stand in the moment, with a decision before us, very much a part of a sinful world, the possibilities of sin are all around us. In addition, human history is filled with people just like us, choosing sin. Our own personal history is just the same, and all of this presses upon us in this moment. As Kierkegaard put it, since the possibilities of sin are much more possible to us since Adam, eventually "the whole world seems to conspire to make a man guilty."[53]

But, once sin has occurred, and the sinner has become guilty, yet another form of anxiety occurs. For the guilty person is immediately confronted with a new decision: to persist in evil or [by repentance] to begin a

---

53. Kierkegaard, *Concept of Anxiety*, p. 109. Cf. Dupré, *Kierkegaard*, p. 63.

new life. This means that "anxiety reappears in double form: anxiety over evil and anxiety over good."[54]

4.6 Anxiety About Evil

Anxiety about evil is worse for us than for Adam, since we now know that sin is in the world. We know evil and we know its consequences. We know what it is to sin, and we know — at least in the experience of those before us — what it is to die. It is a strange thing about human beings that this does not restrain our sinfulness, but instead it simply confirms us in it. As guilty people we are weak (cf. Rom. 5:6), and we are caught up in the objective anxiety of this fallen world, and the subjective anxiety of our own moment before sin, in which we know our own previous failings and the failings of other human beings before us and around us, and in this deadly combination we sin again.[55] "At the maximum we find here the dreadful fact that *anxiety about sin produces sin*."[56]

According to Kierkegaard, this is one of the most dangerous aspects of moralism, with its persistent attention to identifying sin and challenging people to be done with it.[57] We shouldn't really need Kierkegaard to teach us this point. The Gospel of John tells us, "This is the verdict: Light has come into the world, but men loved darkness instead of light because their deeds were evil" (John 3:19). The apostle Paul tells us, "Indeed I would not have known what sin was except through the law. For I would not have known what coveting really was if the law had not said, 'Do not covet'" (Rom. 7:7). Anxiety allures us into evil, and a great emphasis on sin is dangerous because it arouses anxiety and so, despite the good intentions of the moralist, it will actually *increase* the sin.[58] Sinners don't really need to hear any more about their sin; they need to hear about God's solution to it.

To reinforce Kierkegaard's point here, it is worthwhile remembering that the NT views repentance preeminently as a turning *toward God* (which, as a reflex, entails also turning from sin), but the moralist mistakenly depicts it in the first place as a turning *from sin*. Evangelical repen-

---

54. Dupré, *Kierkegaard*, p. 64.
55. Kierkegaard, *Concept of Anxiety*, pp. 113-14.
56. Kierkegaard, *Concept of Anxiety*, p. 73.
57. Dupré, *Kierkegaard*, p. 64.
58. Dupré, *Kierkegaard*, p. 62.

tance is provoked by the proclamation of the gospel of what God has done for us in Christ; but the moralist believes it is provoked by a greater awareness of human sin.

To return to Kierkegaard: If repentance is conceived of as a turning from sin, rather than a turning to God, then the sinner is not without danger even in the moment of repentance. For if repentance is from *sin*,[59] then, in Kierkegaard's words:

> Repentance is reduced to a possibility in relation to sin; in other words, repentance cannot cancel sin, it can only sorrow over it. Sin advances in its consequence; repentance follows it step by step, but always a moment too late. It forces itself to look at the dreadful [=what arouses anxiety], but [. . .] it has lost the reins of government, and it has retained only the power to grieve. At this point, anxiety is at its highest.[60]

4.7 Anxiety About the Good ("Demonic Anxiety")

Guilty sinners are also confronted with a second form of anxiety. Not only are we anxious about the evil, but we are also anxious about the good. This anxiety is even more appalling, and Kierkegaard calls it "demonic anxiety."[61] Just as sinners are enslaved to sin, so, too, we are enslaved to not being able to choose the good.[62] Here we show that we actually live in unfreedom.

Kierkegaard explains the anxiety about the good by referring to the account of the man with the unclean spirit in the Capernaum synagogue (Mark 1:21-28). As Jesus begins teaching so wonderfully, the unclean spirit rises up against him and says, "What have you to do with us, Jesus of Nazareth?" (τί ἡμῖν καί σοί, Mark 1:24).[63] In the presence of the very incarnation

---

59. "The posited sin is an unwarranted actuality. It is posited as an actuality in repentance" (Kierkegaard, *Concept of Anxiety*, p. 115). For a discussion of *evangelical* repentance, see R. C. Doyle, "Repentance," in *Responding to the Gospel: Evangelical Perspectives on Christian Living*, ed. B. G. Webb (Adelaide: Openbook Publishers, 1995).

60. Kierkegaard, *Concept of Anxiety*, p. 115.

61. Kierkegaard's discussion of the demoniacal is "one of the most remarkable studies ever written on that subject" (Dupré, *Kierkegaard*, p. 65).

62. Kierkegaard, *Concept of Anxiety*, p. 123.

63. Kierkegaard, *Concept of Anxiety*, p. 123.

of goodness, the demoniac closes himself off from the good. This is demonic anxiety, and it is not just the demons who experience it. Demonic anxiety about the good is also a feature of fallen humanity.

Anxiety about the good is "even more dangerous" than anxiety about the evil. For it shuts a person up from the good,[64] making them a prisoner in their unfreedom, and so takes them toward despair.[65] Kierkegaard calls this situation "inclosing reserve,"[66] or, what someone else has described as "inwardness with a closed lock."[67] For demonic anxiety incloses a person on themselves and removes them from real communication with the "outside world." The kind of reserve he is talking about is not a kind of reclusive silence, it is instead the absence of any real communication with the world that assists a person to move toward becoming spirit. The person in demonic anxiety doesn't stop talking; in fact, they may be bubbling over with speech, but the point is that this speech is not really meaningful.[68] In fact, it is related to boredom.[69]

Perhaps there is an analogy here with the kind of speech psychologists might call "the chronicle," which "reflects a state of disconnection from inner experience" and is "told in a relationship of disconnection."[70]

> The clinical chronicle is, characteristically, a catalogue of problems with the family, with work, and of symptoms. Nothing comes from the interior world. The individual's experience is dominated by events, the language is linear, and there is a relative poverty of metaphoric usage. Furthermore, there is no pleasure in the conversation. The chronicling conveys a sense of deadness, without creative aliveness.[71]

---

64. "Shut-upness is for Kierkegaard the most adequate expression of evil" (Dupré, *Kierkegaard*, p. 65).

65. Dupré, *Kierkegaard*, p. 64.

66. Kierkegaard, *Concept of Anxiety*, pp. 123, 126.

67. *The Sickness unto Death: A Christian Psychological Exposition for Upbuilding and Awakening*, ed. and trans. H. V. and E. H. Hong (Princeton: Princeton University Press, 1983), p. 72.

68. "Rather than alienation, language provides the possibility of intimacy" (Meares, *Intimacy and Alienation*, p. 121).

69. P. Bigelow, *Kierkegaard and the Problem of Writing* (Tallahassee: University Presses of Florida, 1987), p. 124.

70. Meares, *Intimacy and Alienation*, p. 124.

71. Meares, *Intimacy and Alienation*, p. 123. The two alternative types of conversation in a clinical therapy situation are the narrative and the script.

Demonic anxiety increasingly cuts a person off from continuity with the flow of human community, shunning every contact with the good.[72] In God's relationally constructed universe, this, of course, keeps them from becoming spirit, the person God wants them to be.

Alongside the death of his father, the other great defining moment of Kierkegaard's life was when he broke off his engagement with Regine Olsen. His writings return to this action time and time again. Despite how often he discusses it, his reasons for breaking the engagement remain rather mysterious, and it is a favorite game among Kierkegaard scholars to try to discover them.[73] Without entering into this game, or trying to suggest that this is the only reason, perhaps "anxiety about the good" was at least in part responsible for this heart-wrenching decision Kierkegaard had to take responsibility for throughout the rest of his life.[74]

And so, these are the two kinds of subjective anxiety we experience in this fallen world: anxiety about the evil, and anxiety about the good.

After such a lengthy discussion, it is clear that Kierkegaard — like the New Testament — saw anxiety as a part of life that was definitely here to stay in this fallen world. However, in the same way that all things can work together for the good of those who love God (Rom. 8:28), so, too, anxiety can serve a positive good, in that it provides an opportunity not just for sin, but for faith.

4.8 Anxiety and Faith

Even though we live in a fallen world in the midst of both objective and subjective anxiety, experiencing anxiety about the evil and anxiety about the good, we still have the task to become spirit. Our anxiety-ridden context is an opportunity to exercise faith, by which we are saved and anxiety

72. Kierkegaard, *Concept of Anxiety*, p. 129: "*The demonic is the sudden.* [. . .] Inclosing reserve increasingly cuts itself off from communication, and communication is continuity, and the negation of continuity is the sudden."

73. E. H. Duncan, *Søren Kierkegaard* (Waco, TX: Word Books), pp. 23-24: Was it the difference in age? Was it an early experience he had with a prostitute, like the story in *Either/Or?* Or was this experience his father's, and he could not reveal this to Regine? Or was it simply that marriage would interfere with his writing, which he saw as his divine mission?; — the last being Duncan's own view.

74. For a brief description of these events, see Watts, *Kierkegaard,* pp. 31-38.

is transformed into grace.[75] Whereas despair is an entirely negative thing for Kierkegaard, anxiety is not, for it can become the doorway for faith and so salvation.[76]

For Kierkegaard, faith is personal appropriation of and commitment to God's saving work in Jesus Christ.[77] Anxiety always has this as a possible outcome, and human existence ought to be a constant striving toward the person God wants us to be, which we attain in Christ and only beyond the temporal sphere.[78]

Alluding to the Grimm's fairy tale known as "The Youth Who Went Forth to Learn What Fear Was," Kierkegaard comments that

> this is an adventure that every human being must go through — to learn to be anxious in order that he may not perish either by never having been in anxiety or by succumbing in anxiety. Whoever has learned to be anxious in the right way has learned the ultimate.[79]

He who in relation to guilt is educated by anxiety will rest only in the Atonement.[80] And that, of course, is faith.

4.9 Anxiety and Evangelical Joy

When it is used properly within God's purposes to make us into the persons we were created to be, then anxiety issues in evangelical joy. In contrast to the "inclosing reserve" of the despairing sinner, the sinner who stands before the goodness of God in faith wants to move from his or her anxiety toward the fullness of life that the gospel promises — no matter how threatening this may feel.

> One cannot be inclosed in God or in the good, because this kind of inclosure signifies the greatest expansion.[81]

---

75. Dupré, *Kierkegaard*, p. 65. The alternative is to choose despair, that is, to refuse to be your real self.

76. Pattison, *Kierkegaard*, p. 103.

77. Gardiner, *Kierkegaard*, p. 103.

78. Gardiner, *Kierkegaard*, p. 109.

79. Kierkegaard, *Concept of Anxiety*, p. 155.

80. Kierkegaard, *Concept of Anxiety*, p. 162.

81. Kierkegaard, *Concept of Anxiety*, pp. 133-34.

Kierkegaard, like Hamlet before him, has been called "the melancholy Dane,"[82] but this is to tell only half the story, and probably comes from the all-too-common practice of severing his ideas from their Christian moorings. Yes, he spoke of his unhappy childhood, and his adult life was also filled with its many traumas and sufferings. But in the midst of the difficulties of life, Kierkegaard's meditation upon anxiety can bring us the consolation of a deep, evangelical joy.[83] Anxiety is not something to flee from; but it is here, in the midst of the anxiety that is built into the fabric of our fallen world, that we can hear the promises of the gospel most sharply. It is here I am summoned to believe, to stake my all on the Son of God who loved me and gave himself up for me (Gal. 2:20).

5. The Age of Anxiety and the Quest for Security

So how has Søren Kierkegaard helped us to reflect upon the teaching of the New Testament on anxiety? This final section weaves his insights with the Scriptural teaching, allowing a richer understanding of the anxiety in which we are destined to live.

5.1 This Is the Age of Anxiety

This is the age of anxiety. There is no way around that. The objective anxiety delivered to our world by Adam's fall means that there is a profound insecurity that is all around us, and everywhere in us. Our mortality makes us insecure, and it is all too easy to succumb to anxiety about ordinary life: what we eat, what we drink, and what we wear. Extraordinary threats to life are always with us, and it is all too easy to succumb to anxiety about these extraordinary dangers to ourselves and those we love. The fall has also

---

82. P. T. Forsyth, *The Work of Christ* (London: Independent, 1938, repr. 1952 [original: 1910]), p. xxxii, refers to Kierkegaard as "the great and melancholy Dane in whom Hamlet was mastered by Christ." This epithet then becomes the subtitle for Martin's book, *Kierkegaard: The Melancholy Dane*. See p. 10.

83. Kierkegaard's own evangelical joy is quite frequently expressed in his prayers (LeFevre, *Prayers*), his sermons *(Edifying Discourses)*, and in his journal entries (A. Dru, trans. and ed., *The Journals of Kierkegaard* [New York: Harper & Row, 1959]; P. P. Rohde, ed., *The Diary of Søren Kierkegaard* [New York: Philosophical Library, 1960]).

brought us a history of human sinfulness both out there in the lives of others, and in here in my own personal history. When faced with a moment of decision, it is all too easy to be anxious about the evil. And sin has so distorted us that we are also anxious about the good. God's ways aren't viewed as freedom, but as slavery; and God's promised expansion and enrichment of life can be perceived as a bad thing, rather than a good. It is all too easy to succumb to anxiety about the good, and so contract and restrict into the inclosing reserve of demonic anxiety.

The danger is that we experience this anxiety and, like the seeds in the thorny ground, the word of God is choked and we are choked in the process.

But the gospel needs to be constantly heard. Not only is this the age of anxiety, it is also the age of the Messiah.

5.2 This Is the Age of the Messiah

The time is fulfilled. The kingdom of God has drawn near. Jesus Christ has lived and died, and risen from the dead. Because of the Messiah, human beings can come back to the Father. They can find rest for their souls. The birds of the air and the lilies of the field can provide important lessons for us. Jesus Christ has brought us back to the Father. The Father cares for us more than the birds and the lilies. In our anxiety, we can pray. We can turn to him and cast our anxieties on his lap, because he cares for us. In fact, if we face our anxiety properly, as an experience that is designed in God's plan to leave us resting more firmly on him in faith, then we can live in this age of anxiety with a deep evangelical joy.

5.3 This Is the Age of Anxious Longing for the Redemption of Our Bodies

And our anxiety actually becomes transformed into hope.

The anxious longing of creation will only be removed on that great day of resurrection. Until that time, we are destined to live in this age of anxiety. The creation has been subjected to futility, and it groans all around us. As part of this creation, human beings groan at their core, the anxious longing of creation being manifest in the profound soul-deep disjuncture that is the fear of death. When the Spirit of God comes to a person because they are justified through the work of Christ, this only adds to the groaning. For the Spirit is the Spirit of resurrection, the down payment of the good things to come, and the Spirit begins to groan along with our spirits, anxiously longing for the redemption of our bodies on that great day of resurrection.

5.4 *In Our Anxiety, Here Is God's Security*

Because of Jesus Christ, nothing will take that future away. If anxiety is aroused by the possibilities, then here is something that is not actually present yet, but is as sure as if it were. Jesus Christ has died, and yes, he has risen from the dead. If he has risen from the dead, then we, too, will one day rise from the dead. The anxious longing of creation is groaning toward that resurrection in front of us, with the certainty that comes from having a resurrection already behind us.

Here is God's security. Nothing can separate us from the love of God. Nothing in ordinary life. Nothing in the ordinary relationships of life. None of the extraordinary threats to life. Not even the massive disruption brought to our creation when sin entered the world and death through sin. Not even the presence or possibility of our own sin. Nothing can separate us from the love of God in Christ Jesus. And that means, despite our multi-faceted anxiety, the future is sure.

In this way, the gospel promises bring us the most profound consolation. With the promise of this glorious future, even in the midst of the groans of our anxious world, there is a tremendous impetus to constantly turn our own groans into prayers — to "cast all your anxieties upon him because he cares for you" (1 Pet. 5:7).

Bibliography

Australian Government, *Mental Health: A Report Focussing on Depression*, http://www.health.gov.au/internet/wcms/publishing.nsf/content/health-mediarel-yr1999-mw-hmc5.htm (5th May 2006).

Australian Government, http://www.health.gov.au/internet/wcms/publishing.nsf/Content/health-archivemediare1-1998-mw4398.htm (5th May 2006).

Bigelow, P. *Kierkegaard and the Problem of Writing.* Tallahassee: University Presses of Florida, 1987.

Bolt, P. G. *Jesus' Defeat of Death: Persuading Mark's Early Readers.* SNTSMS 125. Cambridge: Cambridge University Press, 2003.

Bouwsma, W. J. "The Durable Renaissance: Anxiety and the Formation of Early Modern Culture," in William J. Bouwsma, *A Usable Past: Essays in European Cultural History.* Berkeley : University of California Press, 1990, pp. 157-89.

Dodds, E. R. *Pagan and Christian in an Age of Anxiety: Some Aspects of Religious Experience from Marcus Aurelius to Constantine.* Cambridge: University Press, 1965.

Doyle, R. C. "Repentance," in *Responding to the Gospel: Evangelical Perspectives on Christian Living,* edited by B. G. Webb. Adelaide: Openbook Publishers, 1995, pp. 15-39.

Dru, A., trans. and ed. *The Journals of Kierkegaard.* New York: Harper & Row, 1959 [1938].

DSM IV. *Diagnostic and Statistical Manual of Mental Disorders, 4th Edition.* Washington, D.C.: American Psychiatric Association, 1994, 71998.

Duncan, E. H. *Søren Kierkegaard.* Waco, TX: Word Books, p. 197.

Dupré, L. *Kierkegaard the Theologian: The Dialectic of Christian Existence.*New York: Sheed & Ward, 1963.

Edelman, S. *Change Your Thinking.* Sydney: ABC Books, 2002.

Forsyth, P. T. *The Work of Christ.* London: Independent, 1938, repr. 1952 [original: 1910].

Gardiner, P. L. *Kierkegaard.* Oxford: Oxford University Press, 1988.

Garff, J. *Søren Kierkegaard: A Biography.* Translated by B. H. Kirmmse. Princeton and Oxford: Princeton University Press, 2005 [Danish: 2000].

Gerzon, R. *Finding Serenity in the Age of Anxiety.* New York: Macmillan, 1997.

Hannay, A. *Kierkegaard: A Biography.* Cambridge: Cambridge University Press, 2001.

Kierkegaard, S. *The Sickness unto Death: A Christian Psychological Exposition for Upbuilding and Awakening.* Edited, translated, and introduced by H. V. and E. H. Hong. Princeton: Princeton University Press, 1983.

Kierkegaard, S. *Kierkegaard's The Concept of Dread.* Translated by W. Lowrie. Princeton: Princeton University Press, 1944.

Kierkegaard, S. *The Concept of Anxiety: A Simple Psychologically Orienting Deliberation on the Dogmatic Issue of Hereditary Sin.* Edited and translated by R. Thomte and A. B. Anderson. Princeton: Princeton University Press, 1980.

Kierkegaard, S. *Edifying Discourses: A Selection.* Edited by P. L. Holmer. Translated by D. F. and L. M. Swenson. London: Collins, Fontana, 1958.

LeFevre, P. D., ed. *The Prayers of Kierkegaard.* Chicago: University of Chicago Press, 1956.

Lowrie, W. *Kierkegaard.* 2 vols. Oxford: Oxford University Press, 1938; New York: Harper & Row, 1962.

MacDonald, M. *Mystical Bedlam: Madness, Anxiety and Healing in Seventeenth-Century England.* Cambridge: Cambridge University Press, 1983.

Magurshak, D. "The Concept of Anxiety: A Keystone of the Kierkegaard — Heidegger Relationship," in R. L. Perkins, ed., *The International Kierkegaard Commentary: The Concept of Anxiety.* Macon, Ga.: Mercer University Press, 1985, pp. 167-95.

Martin, H. V. *Kierkegaard: The Melancholy Dane.* London: Epworth, 1950.

McRillis, N. R. "Atomic Anxiety in Cold War Britain: Science, Sin, and Uncertainty in Nuclear Monster Films," in George Aichele and Richard Walsh, eds., *Screening Scripture: Intertextual Connections Between Scripture and Film.* Harrisburg, Pa.: Trinity Press International, 2002, pp. 42-57.

Meares, R. *Intimacy and Alienation: Memory, Trauma and Personal Being.* London and Philadelphia: Routledge, 2000.

Nuth, J. M. *God's Lovers in an Age of Anxiety: The Medieval English Mystics.* London: Darton, Longman & Todd, 2001.

Palmer, D. *Kierkegaard for Beginners.* London: Writers and Readers Limited, 1996.

Pattison, G. *Kierkegaard and the Crisis of Faith: An Introduction to His Thought.* London: SPCK, 1997.

Peck, M. S. *The Road Less Traveled and Beyond: Spiritual Growth in an Age of Anxiety.* London: Rider, 1997.

Robinson, D. and O. Zarate. *Introducing Kierkegaard.* Duxford, U.K.: Icon, 2003.

Rohde, P. P., ed. *The Diary of Søren Kierkegaard.* New York: Philosophical Library, 1960.

Rohr, R. and J. B. Feister. *Hope Against Darkness: The Transforming Vision of Saint Francis in an Age of Anxiety.* Cincinnati: St. Anthony Messenger Press, 2001.

Rossinow, D. *The Politics of Authenticity: Liberalism, Christianity, and the New Left in America.* New York: Columbia University Press, 1998.

Watts, M. *Kierkegaard* .Oxford: Oneworld, 2003.

Wengst, K. *Pax Romana and the Peace of Jesus Christ.* Translated by J. Bowden. London: SCM, 1987 [German: 1986].

Zuckermann, A. J. "Judaism and the Age of Anxiety," in S. A. Burrell, ed., *The Role of Religion in Modern European History.* New York: Macmillan, 1964, pp. 133-40.

BONHOEFFER
on Disappointment

Brian S. Rosner

Hope does not disappoint.

Romans 5:5a

Golf was once described as a long walk punctuated by disappointments, and a football fan as someone who, no matter what the score, is in a constant state of disappointment. Somewhat histrionically, Anne of Green Gables complained: "My life is a perfect graveyard of buried hopes."[1] Disappointment is such a universal human experience that one American wit, Ambrose Bierce, defined a year as "a period of three hundred and sixty-five disappointments" and the "present" as "that part of eternity dividing the domain of disappointment from the realm of hope." According to George Orwell's *Animal Farm*, "the unalterable law of life [is] . . . hunger, hardship and disappointment."[2] It seems that no one is immune from the displeasure caused by having their hopes or expectations unfulfilled.

Of course some disappointments are worse than others. It is one thing to be sad about a tied score, or a low mark on a term paper, or a wet picnic on a public holiday; it is quite another to bear the distress of long-term unemployment, unrequited or unfulfilled love, a couple's infertility, or the setback of a serious illness with all the attendant frustrations. You can re-

---

1. L. M. Montgomery, *Anne of Green Gables*, chapter 5.
2. George Orwell, *Animal Farm*, chapter 10, p. 109.

cover from a disappointment with a serving of your favorite dessert, or it could lead to a midlife crisis, a destructive addiction, or a deep depression. Indeed, disappointments can be fleeting and trivial or chronic and profound, grave, and bitter. Dietrich Bonhoeffer's were definitely of the latter sort, and it is for this very reason, as we shall see, that his response to disappointment is so inspiring and instructive.

The magnitude of any given disappointment must be measured in two directions. First, the *height of anticipation* can set you up for a big letdown. It is harder to cope with the disappointment of your team losing the grand final if you have been waiting for the moment for decades. In the same way, it is harder to live in a tiny studio apartment if you grew up in a palace. The single person who puts great stock on getting married will find it harder to manage when they don't find Mr. or Miss Right than the person who expects less from a change in marital status.

Secondly, the *depth of failure* increases the chagrin of disappointment. When eating out, if you were hoping for goose on the menu, you can easily cope with the disappointment of being served duck. Conversely, it is harder to handle if you fossick for gold and find only sand.

Major Disappointment = High Hopes + Dismal Failure
Minor Disappointment = Inconsequential Hopes + Negligible Failure

The most profound disappointments are those that combine both a great height of anticipation and a severe depth of failure. Tragically, Bonhoeffer's life was distinguished by precisely these two elements: prodigious prospects and devastating failure.

How did Dietrich Bonhoeffer handle his disappointments? Although he wrote a number of books, the answer to this question is found in the remarkable letters to and from his parents, relatives, fiancée, and above all his best friend Eberhard Bethge, collected and published in the now classic volumes *Letters and Papers from Prison* and *Love Letters from Cell 92*.[3] We

---

3. *Letters and Papers from Prison* was first published in German in 1951. Three English editions, each including new material, appeared in 1953, 1967, and 1971. Not surprisingly, for decades Bonhoeffer's surviving fiancée declined to release their letters. Shortly before her death in 1977 she finally acceded to the many requests and entrusted their correspondence to her sister for publication: *Love Letters from Cell 92: Dietrich Bonhoeffer and Maria von Wedemeyer*, ed. Ruth-Alice von Bismarck and Ulrich Kabitz, trans. John Brownjohn (London: HarperCollins, 1994).

read these books with a real sense of privilege, especially seeing most of the letters were smuggled in and out of prison at considerable risk. Bonhoeffer himself described the letters as "the miracle of the correspondence."[4] The original German title of *Letters and Papers from Prison* captures the poignancy of the material for a study of disappointment: *Widerstand und Ergebung* — "Resistance and Surrender." We might paraphrase it: "Hope and Failure."

For the purpose of comparison, readers would do well to recall an important disappointment in their own lives and how they dealt with or are dealing with it. Disappointment can be either past or present, involving the loss of former happiness or the ache of as-yet-unfulfilled hopes. Where do you find comfort and consolation in the face of real disappointment? The concept of disappointment overlaps with and may lead to a number of related problems and experiences, including frustration, yearning, anger, envy, nostalgia, suffering, desire, discouragement, despair, and loss. Above all, seeking consolation for disappointment involves learning how to cope with setbacks and maintain hope.

Great Expectations

Dietrich Bonhoeffer was born on 4 February 1906, along with his twin sister, Sabine, in Breslau, Germany, the sixth of eight children. His family had been prominent in German society for centuries, with many doctors, lawyers, judges, and professors among his ancestors. Dietrich's father, Karl, was a professor of psychiatry and his paternal grandfather, Friedrich, had been the president of the Tübingen High Court. On his mother's side, his grandmother, Clara von Hase (née von Kalckreuth), was a countess, his grandfather, Karl von Hase, was a professor of church history and chaplain to Kaiser Wilhelm, and his uncle and great-grandfather were two of Germany's best-known painters. His mother studied piano with Liszt. His older siblings became or married professors, scientists, and lawyers. The family home in Breslau was a mansion in a beautiful forest of birch trees complete with a tennis court, orchard, a huge garden, and a menagerie of animals. The staff included a cook, a housemaid, a parlor maid, a governess, a French governess, a chauffeur, a receptionist, and a gardener. In

---

4. *Letters and Papers from Prison* (New York: Touchstone, 1997), p. 315.

Berlin, where the family moved in Dietrich's sixth year, the Bonhoeffer home was equally grand. The dining table could seat twenty people and the reception room had a Bechstein grand piano, oriental carpets, and paintings of the Alps and famous relatives by famous relatives. They also owned a summerhouse in the Harz mountains. From any angle, Dietrich Bonhoeffer was marked for greatness.

For all his privileges and opportunities, it was not as if Bonhoeffer's childhood was always wrapped in cotton wool. World War I saw not only the defeat of the German nation but the loss of Dietrich's brother Walter and the nervous breakdown of his mother. Nonetheless, to use the words Dietrich wrote from prison for his godson's baptism, he came from a home that "had pride in public service, intellectual achievement and leadership, and a deep-rooted sense of duty towards a great heritage and cultural tradition."[5]

Dietrich was a tall man, with an athletic physique, and a round boyish face. With his mother's blue eyes and blond hair, he fitted perfectly Hitler's Aryan stereotype. He was unusual by the normally aloof German professorial standards in that he swam and played tennis with his students. He had a love of travel, spending extended periods outside Germany, including study in Italy, North Africa, and America, and pastoral charges in Barcelona and London. His work with the World Alliance of Churches also saw him visit many other countries.[6]

High Hopes Dashed

Two aspirations dominated Bonhoeffer's life — one national, the other personal: (1) Dietrich worked for the renewal of the German church and people; and (2) he planned to marry his fiancée, Maria von Wedemeyer. Both desires were cruelly thwarted in 1943 when he was arrested by the Gestapo, incarcerated for two years, and finally executed at the order of Adolf Hitler.

Dietrich's opposition to the Nazis commenced from a few days after Hitler first took power in 1933 when he gave an abruptly ended radio broadcast on the dangers of charismatic leadership. For the next ten years

5. *Letters and Papers from Prison*, p. 294.
6. Theodore J. Kleinhans, *Till the Night Be Past: The Life and Times of Dietrich Bonhoeffer* (St. Louis: Concordia, 2002), p. 170, lists seventeen countries that Bonhoeffer visited in his lifetime, in Europe, the Americas, and North Africa.

he worked for the good of his nation, eventually operating as a double agent and even taking part in the plots to kill Hitler. Imbued with a strong sense of vocation, Bonhoeffer felt his detainment not only as a private setback; he regarded it as a blow to this larger cause. He wrote to Bethge: "I feel that my own personal future is of quite secondary importance compared with the general situation, though, of course, the two things are very closely related."[7] When he reminisced to Bethge in January 1944, "we had many good hopes," he was referring to the failed overthrow of March 1943 that had led to his arrest.[8] His mother wrote to him: I understand your "incomprehension about your situation . . . when you have to look on ineffectually and cannot help anyone, in the best years of your manhood."[9] In one of his last surviving letters Dietrich expressed his conviction that "the church must come out of its stagnation."[10]

Bonhoeffer wrote a number of poems from prison arising from reflections on his desperate circumstances. "The Death of Moses"[11] reveals his sadness about missing out on the future reconstruction of Christian life in postwar Germany. Dietrich identified with Moses' deep disappointment; the ancient prophet had led God's people through the wilderness to the verge of the Promised Land only to be refused entry:

On the heights where no one goes,
to him, the promised land God shows.

Spread beneath the wanderer's tired feet,
lies the home he longs to greet.

. . .

Holy land, to me you have appeared,
like a bejeweled bride, lovely and endeared,

the bridal dress lights up your virgin face,
your bridal jewels are of costly grace.

7. *Letters and Papers from Prison*, p. 239.
8. *Letters and Papers from Prison*, p. 183.
9. *Letters and Papers from Prison*, p. 102.
10. *Letters and Papers from Prison*, p. 378.
11. *The Prison Poems of Dietrich Bonhoeffer: A New Translation and Commentary*, ed. and trans. Edwin Robertson (Guilford, U.K.: Eagle, 1998), pp. 82-89.

. . .

You who punish sin and forgive readily,
God, you know I have loved this people steadily.

That I have born their shame and sacrifice
and seen their salvation — will suffice.

Hold, support me, I lose my stave,
faithful God, prepare me for my grave.

The poem is about Moses, but the resonances with Dietrich's own tragic experience are unmistakable.

If Bonhoeffer could compare the goal of a restored Germany to a lovely bride, his most personal aspiration was the literal fulfillment of this image. In June 1942 Dietrich visited Frau Ruth von Kleist-Retzow, a generous supporter of his work over many years. One of her granddaughters, Maria von Wedemeyer, was present. Dietrich and Maria fell in love. Maria was "beautiful, . . . poised, fresh, cultured, filled with vitality,"[12] but only eighteen years of age, fully seventeen years younger than Dietrich! Maria's father had been killed on the Russian Front and her mother insisted on a year's separation to test the couple's feelings. Maria convinced her mother otherwise and in January 1943, with some restrictions in place, they were engaged to be married.

Needless to say, Bonhoeffer's arrest and imprisonment on April 5th was a bitter blow. Uncannily, without knowledge, Maria wrote in her diary on that very day: "Has something bad happened? I'm afraid it must be something very bad."[13] In his first letter from prison to his parents Dietrich wrote: "You can imagine that I'm most particularly anxious about my fiancée at the moment. It's a great deal for her to bear."[14] In fact from that point on most of his letters to relatives and friends from prison mention Maria, who ultimately became the symbol of Dietrich's hopes: "I am forced to live from the past; the future which announces itself in the person of Maria still consists so very much of hints that it lies more on the horizon of hope than in the realm of possession and tangible experi-

12. Kleinhans, *Till the Night Be Past*, p. 149.
13. *Love Letters*, p. 11.
14. *Letters and Papers*, p. 22.

ence."[15] The resolute man of daunting intellect and courageous action was head over heels in love. He wrote that his relationship with Maria led him to recognize "strong personal feeling and real yearning" after having lived "many years absorbed in aims and tasks and hopes without any personal longings."[16] Six months into his incarceration he could still effuse to his friend: "Maria is astounding!"[17] His frustration in prison was palpable. He complained to Bethge: "We've now been engaged almost a year, and so far we haven't spent even an hour alone together."[18]

For Maria, the situation was no easier. Twelve agonizing months into his imprisonment she wrote: "Sometimes when I wake up in the night and can't help thinking of you so much, I wonder if I've been woken by a thought of yours. And that would be lovely. When I get up at half-past five in the morning, I always try to think of you very gently and cautiously, so as to let you sleep on a bit. I've chalked a line around my bed roughly the size of your cell. There are a table and chair standing there, the way I picture it, and when I sit there I almost believe I'm with you. If only I really were."[19]

The pain of their separation can be felt acutely throughout their letters. In her first letter to Dietrich in prison Maria wrote about her work as a nurse's aid and her infatuation with the name Dietrich: "While I'm dressing the four little children in my care, I tell them stories about 'Uncle Dietrich.' When I'm scrubbing and polishing, I think, 'Dietrich, Dietrich' in time to my movements. And, when I discuss first names with my women's ward, you can be sure they all agree that 'Dietrich' is the nicest."[20]

Around sixty-five of Maria's letters to Dietrich in prison survive. Even the way she addressed them gives some idea of the intensity of their love and the pain of their separation. Four begin with "Dear Dietrich," one with "Dear, dear Dietrich," three with "My dear, dear Dietrich," one with "My very dearest Dietrich," two with "My one dear Dietrich," eleven with "Dearest Dietrich," and twenty-six with "My dearest Dietrich." Other variations include, once "My beloved Dietrich," twice "My dearly beloved

---

15. *Letters and Papers*, p. 160.
16. *Letters and Papers*, p. 271.
17. *Letters and Papers*, p. 132.
18. *Letters and Papers*, p. 162.
19. *Love Letters*, p. 227.
20. *Love Letters*, p. 23.

Dietrich," twice "My most beloved Dietrich," once "My very dear, beloved Dietrich," and my favorite, twice "My beloved you!"

Prison for Bonhoeffer was a horrendous ordeal. However, he was not given to self-pity. He wrote to Bethge: "When people suggest in their letters . . . that I'm suffering here, I reject the thought."[21] At other points, nonetheless, he still describes his imprisonment as "this nightmare"[22] and as "absolutely demoralizing in every possible way."[23] He wrote ominously: "My grim experiences often pursue me into the night"[24] — "this waiting is revolting."[25] The first eighteen months were spent in Tegel Prison in Berlin, from which almost all of the surviving correspondence originated. One cannot help but contrast the salubrious surroundings of his childhood in Breslau and Berlin. Dietrich's general fitness saved him from serious illness, although he did report the stone floors aggravating his lumbago, rheumatism, and bouts of influenza. Air raids and interrogations proved trying. Like any good Continental European he complains about the bad coffee and poor tobacco. At different points he writes of wanting to "see the sun" and "experience it bodily" and of longing for "a glass of Berlin beer."[26] His letters are littered with allusions to European culture, music, architecture, and art. In his view, "the mind's hunger for discussion is much more tormenting than the body's hunger for food."[27] He read diligently a wide of range of literature in German, French, Latin, Greek, and English, everything from academic theology to poetry and novels to English grammar and a history of Scotland Yard, and especially the Bible several times through. At his most optimistic he could say: "I'm getting on all right, working and waiting."[28]

21. *Letters and Papers*, p. 232.
22. *Letters and Papers*, p. 72.
23. *Letters and Papers*, p. 64.
24. *Letters and Papers*, p. 162.
25. *Letters and Papers*, p. 164.
26. *Letters and Papers*, p. 340.
27. *Letters and Papers*, p. 177.
28. *Letters and Papers*, p. 195.

Dealing with Disappointment

Popular Strategies

The pain of disappointment can be dealt with in a number of ways psychologically and religiously. Some people are regretful at making choices that have led to the non-fulfillment of their hopes. Others succumb to curbing the desire for what they had previously wanted in order to lessen the pain of the loss. Still others seek compensation elsewhere, in some substitute or in a form of distraction. A specifically religious response is simply to look forward to compensation in the life to come. Somewhat surprisingly, Bonhoeffer opposes all these strategies and finds in them no real consolation. He refused to wallow in regret, curb his desires, seek a substitute, or just give up and wait for the resurrection from the dead.

First, he did not wallow in regret. Bonhoeffer had every reason to feel remorseful at decisions he had made that led to his wretched imprisonment. We might feel the same about choices we have made that have caused adverse consequences and missed opportunities. The most obvious one in Dietrich's case was his resolve in 1939 not to stay in the safe environment of America but to return to Germany, as he put it, in order to "be involved in Germany's fate."[29] In prison he wrote: "I'm often surprised how little (in contrast to nearly all the others here) I grub among my past mistakes and think how different one thing or another would be today if I had acted differently in the past. It doesn't worry me at all."[30] At first blush this may seem arrogant. But Bonhoeffer does not consider himself infallible. On the contrary, he cherishes the forgiveness of his sins. The sermon he wrote from prison for Eberhard and Renate Bethge's wedding includes the words: "live together in the forgiveness of your sins, for without it no human fellowship . . . can survive."[31] Rather, it is his confidence in the sovereign goodness of God that frees him from dwelling morbidly on past mistakes. In his view, "everything seems to be determined necessarily and straightforwardly by a higher providence."[32] At a key juncture he wrote to comfort his dear friend Eberhard Bethge: "Now I want to assure you that I

29. *Letters and Papers*, p. 174.
30. *Letters and Papers*, p. 276.
31. *Letters and Papers*, p. 46.
32. *Letters and Papers*, p. 276.

haven't for a moment regretted coming back in 1939. . . . I knew quite well what I was doing, and I acted with a clear conscience. I've no wish to cross out of my life anything that has happened since, either to me personally or as regards events in general. And I regard my being kept here as being involved in Germany's fate, as I was resolved to be. I don't look back on the past and accept the present reproachfully. . . . All we can do is to live in assurance and faith — you out there with the soldiers, and I in my cell."[33]

Second, he did not curb his desires. It seems only sensible to curb thwarted desires as a kind of self-protection. However, Bonhoeffer will have nothing of it: "To renounce a full life and its real joys in order to avoid pain [or we might say disappointment] is neither Christian nor human."[34] In fact he advocated feeling losses acutely: "Natural composure is probably in most cases nothing but a euphemism for indifference and indolence, and to that extent it's not very estimable. . . . I think we honour God more if we gratefully accept the life that he gives us with all its blessings, loving it and drinking it to the full, and also grieving deeply and sincerely when we have impaired or wasted any of the good things of life."[35]

Third, he did not seek a substitute. Seeking compensation elsewhere when our desires are frustrated also seems logical enough. With respect to separation from loved ones, aware of the pain he may be prolonging, Bonhoeffer nonetheless avers: "Some people . . . find compensation in short-lived pleasures that offer readier satisfaction. . . . When we are forcibly separated for any considerable length of time from those we love, we simply cannot, as most can, get some cheap substitute through other people — I don't mean because of moral considerations. . . . We have to suffer unspeakably from the separation, and feel the longing till it almost makes us ill. That is the only way . . . in which we can preserve unimpaired our relationship with our loved ones."[36] He insists that "nothing can make up for the absence of someone whom we love."[37] Not even God: "It is nonsense to say that God fills the gap; he doesn't fill it, but on the contrary, he keeps it empty and so helps us to keep alive our former communion with each other, even at the cost of pain."[38]

33. *Letters and Papers*, p. 174.
34. *Letters and Papers*, p. 191.
35. *Letters and Papers*, p. 191.
36. *Letters and Papers*, p. 167.
37. *Letters and Papers*, p. 176.
38. *Letters and Papers*, p. 176.

And fourth, he did not give up and simply wait for heaven. Bonhoeffer does not oppose outright anticipating consolation for disappointments in the life to come. In fact he has a very specific notion of the form of this compensation (see below). Rather, in his view, problems arise when we flee too quickly to such comfort: "It is only when one loves life and the earth so much that without them everything seems to be over that one may believe in the resurrection and a new world."[39] To compare the apostle Paul, even if it is true that in Paul's view "to die is gain," nonetheless, life, even a difficult life, is not thereby surrendered, for "to live is Christ" (Phil. 1:21).

Learning from Dietrich Bonhoeffer

In turning to Bonhoeffer for consolation we must tread carefully. In fact, we need to issue a disclaimer. At one point he wrote to Maria: "I know I am awfully bad at saying anything that will cheer and console."[40] One night after a severe air raid certain fellow prisoners approached Dietrich "for a bit of comfort." Concerning this incident he wrote to Eberhard: "But I'm afraid I'm bad at comforting; I can listen all right, but I can hardly ever find anything to say. . . . I've no sympathy with some wrong-headed attempts to explain away distress, because instead of being a comfort, they are the exact opposite. . . . I sometimes think that real comfort must break in just as unexpectedly as the distress."[41]

As long as we remember that there are no easy answers, nonetheless I remain convinced that Bonhoeffer has much to teach us that is genuinely comforting. In Christian terms, to receive comfort from God, which Dietrich patently did, is to be equipped to comfort others. Bonhoeffer would have agreed with Paul, who wrote of "the Father of compassion and the God of all comfort" being able to "comfort us in all our troubles, so that we can comfort those in any trouble with the comfort we ourselves have received from God" (2 Cor. 1:3-4). We may sum up Dietrich's advice to those seeking consolation for disappointment in eight points.

39. *Letters and Papers*, p. 157.
40. *Love Letters*, p. 56.
41. *Letters and Papers*, p. 203.

1. *Focus on the Invaluable*

The first thing to say is that not all disappointments are equal. Desires can be distorted and may need to be trained and redirected. Bonhoeffer's words are timely to twenty-first-century societies that are so sold on consumerism. He urges a re-ordering of priorities: "There is hardly anything that can make one happier than to feel that one counts for something with other people. What matters here is not numbers, but intensity. In the long run, human relationships are the most important thing in life. . . . God uses us in his dealings with others. Everything else is very close to *hubris*. . . . People are more important than anything else in life. That certainly doesn't mean undervaluing the world of things and practical efficiency. But what is the finest book, or picture, or house, or estate, to me, compared to my wife, my parents, or my friend? For many today man is just part of the world of things."[42] Recall that Bonhoeffer knew better than most what it means to abound materially. The value Bonhoeffer places on the supremacy of relationships is a peculiarly Christian emphasis. We do well to test our own hopes against this bar.

2. *Don't Give Up on Your Legitimate Desires*

Bonhoeffer had every reason to give up in prison and accept his fate. He could easily have applied his belief about the universality of providence in a fatalistic way and let go of his hopes and dreams. But he refused to capitulate. "I believe that God is no timeless fate, but that he waits for and answers sincere prayers and responsible actions."[43] Indeed, it was these very convictions that led him in the first place to work so tirelessly and courageously against the Third Reich: "The meaning of free responsibility: It depends on a God who demands responsible action in a bold venture of faith, and who promises forgiveness and consolation to the man who becomes a sinner in that venture."[44] Reminiscent of Martin Luther's ironic encouragement, that when faced with hard decisions we must "sin boldly," Dietrich dared to continue to hope and trust, to plan and dream.

Even in prison, when his case seemed hopeless, he believed in a God

---

42. *Letters and Papers*, p. 386.
43. *Letters and Papers*, p. 11.
44. *Letters and Papers*, p. 6.

who answers prayer: "I'm now praying quite simply for freedom. There is such a thing as a false composure, which is quite unchristian. As Christians, we needn't be at all ashamed of some impatience, longing, opposition to what is unnatural, and our full share of desire for freedom, earthly happiness, and opportunity for effective work."[45] The "Prayers for Fellow Prisoners" that he wrote includes the frank petition: "Restore me to liberty."[46]

3. Embrace a Godly Optimism

Bonhoeffer's approach to prison life was not to allow the confinement to restrict his activity. Quite literally, Dietrich did not sit still while waiting for his hope for freedom to materialize: "I read, meditate, write, pace up and down my cell — without rubbing myself sore against the walls like a polar bear. The great thing is to stick to what one still has and can do — there is still plenty left — and not to be dominated by the thought of what one cannot do, and the feelings of resentment and discontent."[47] This is good advice for anyone facing the frustrations of an ongoing disappointment. Dietrich drew comfort from the Genesis 41:52 description of Joseph's time in jail, who celebrated that "God has made me fruitful in the land of my affliction."[48]

New Year 1943, just a few months before his arrest, Bonhoeffer wrote a series of reflections to his fellow conspirators, entitled "After Ten Years." It was kept safe under the roof beams of the Bonhoeffer family home in Berlin until after the war. In it he admits that "it is wiser [according the world's wisdom] to be pessimistic; . . . [for pessimism] is a way of avoiding disappointment."[49] It is true that if you hope for nothing much, and don't get it, the letdown will be less precipitous. It is only natural then to ask, if you've been frustrated in the past, should you give up your dreams to protect yourself in the future?

In his New Year circular, Bonhoeffer, however, refuses to be pessimistic, even though the goal of removing Hitler looked so unattainable. He went on to explain that there are two kinds of optimism: "It is true that there is a silly, cowardly kind of optimism, which we must condemn. But

45. *Letters and Papers*, pp. 131-32.
46. *Letters and Papers*, p. 141.
47. *Letters and Papers*, p. 39.
48. *Letters and Papers*, p. 234.
49. *Letters and Papers*, p. 15. Italics added.

the optimism that is *will for the future* should never be despised, even if it is proved wrong a hundred times; it is health and vitality, and the sick man has no business to impugn it." With a chilling allusion to the danger the members of the German Resistance faced, Dietrich mused: "It may be that the day of judgment will dawn tomorrow; in that case, we shall gladly stop working for a better future. But not before."[50]

The optimism Bonhoeffer commends and exemplifies, that dogged "will for the future," arises from his conviction that the church is the body of Christ on earth and that that same Christ exists for others.[51] In other words, the church is defined by its "vicarious representative action" on behalf of Christ.[52] For Bonhoeffer to capitulate, to give up his hopes for a better Germany, would be to deny Christ, something he found unthinkable. He was convinced that if "God is for us, who [worth mentioning] can be against us?" (Rom. 8:31). And this thought inspired his godly optimism.

4. Don't Pretend or Minimize the Failure —
Look Disappointment in the Face

For Bonhoeffer, however, it does not follow that to be optimistic is to ignore your frustrations. On the contrary, he struggled to be patient,[53] but believed that "there is a wholeness about the fully grown man which enables him to face an existing situation squarely. We can have an abundant life even though many wishes remain unfulfilled."[54] To Dietrich's mind, "lack of desire is poverty."[55] He asked Bethge insightfully: "Isn't it characteristic of a man, in contrast to an immature person, that his centre of gravity is always where he actually is, and that the longing for the fulfillment of his wishes cannot prevent him from being his whole self?"[56] Bonhoeffer's remarkable resilience was not cultural or constitutional, but

---

50. *Letters and Papers*, pp. 15-16.

51. Cf. his doctoral thesis, *Sanctorum Communio* (subtitle in English: "A dogmatic enquiry into the sociology of the church"), completed in 1927 and published in 1930.

52. Wayne Whitson Floyd, Jr., "Bonhoeffer's Literary Legacy," in *The Cambridge Companion to Dietrich Bonhoeffer,* ed. John W. de Gruchy (Cambridge: Cambridge University Press, 1999), pp. 74-75.

53. *Letters and Papers*, pp. 89-90.

54. *Letters and Papers*, p. 233.

55. *Letters and Papers*, p. 233.

56. *Letters and Papers*, p. 233.

theological. As he wrote to his parents, "'My time is in your hands' (Ps 31) is the Bible's answer [to life's frustrations]."[57]

Bonhoeffer's Christian faith gave him a way of coping with affliction more resolutely. Before his arrest he wrote: "We have to learn that personal suffering is a more effective key, a more rewarding principle for exploring the world in thought and action than personal good fortune."[58] This is not some twisted form of masochism, but the belief that suffering must be endured in solidarity with Christ if we are to live with integrity in this world. The day after the main plot to kill Hitler failed he wrote to console his friend: "By this-worldliness I mean living unreservedly in life's duties, problems, successes and failures, experiences and perplexities. In so doing we throw ourselves completely into the arms of God, taking seriously, not our own sufferings, but those of God in the world — watching with Christ in Gethsemane."[59]

5. Compare Yourself with Those Less Fortunate Rather Than More Fortunate

When things don't work out as you hoped they would, and you find yourself disenchanted and discontent, the natural thing to do is to become self-absorbed, to lose perspective, and to be enveloped in self-pity. Envy is the oxygen to an unhealthy response to disappointment, and envy thrives on comparison. Put simply, Bonhoeffer seems to have avoided this danger by comparing downward, not upward.

He wrote to Bethge: "When people suggest in their letters . . . that I'm 'suffering' here, I reject the thought. . . . I doubt very much whether I'm 'suffering' any more than . . . most people are suffering today."[60] When confronted with terrifying air raids he reasoned: "When the bombs come shrieking down, I always think how trivial it all is compared with what you're going through out there."[61] And he was constantly concerned about and asked after the welfare of his comrades. For instance, he referred in one of his letters to the church leader Martin Niemöller, who had been in Dachau concentration camp since 1937: "Please harbour no regrets about

57. *Letters and Papers*, p. 39.
58. *Letters and Papers*, p. 17.
59. *Letters and Papers*, p. 370.
60. *Letters and Papers*, pp. 231-32.
61. *Letters and Papers*, p. 372.

me. Martin has had nearly seven years of it, and that is a very different matter."[62] (The sad irony is that Niemöller survived the war and Bonhoeffer did not.)

Bonhoeffer continues to feel the pain of others in spite of his own troubles, believing that "the centre of our own lives is outside ourselves."[63] Dietrich's faith enabled him to retain a broader view of his circumstances: "As long as one doesn't lose sight of the greater issues in these small disappointments that one keeps on experiencing, one soon sees how trivial one's own personal privations are."[64]

6. Find Comfort in the God Who "seeks again what is past"

For all his emphasis on living in this world, Bonhoeffer believed profoundly in the life to come. This is nowhere more evident than at his barbaric execution. On 9 April 1945 at Flossenbürg concentration camp he was told to strip naked and then was led away to be hung with piano wire. Captain Payne Best, a British fellow prisoner, reported Dietrich's parting words: "This is the end — for me, the beginning of life."[65]

According to Bonhoeffer, how does future hope help with present disappointment? With reference to experiencing disappointment over the loss of past happiness, as we noted earlier, Bonhoeffer is adamant that it is unwise to flee too quickly to thoughts of compensation in the life to come. He counsels Bethge: that "this poor earth is not our home . . . is indeed something essential, but it must come last of all."[66] Nonetheless in the same letter Dietrich comforts his friend with thoughts derived from Ecclesiastes 3:15, which reads: "God seeks again what is past." Dietrich writes: "I suspect these words mean that nothing that is past is lost, that God gathers up again with us our past, which belongs to us. So when we are seized by a longing for the past — and this may happen when we least expect it — we may be sure that it is only one of the many 'hours' that God is always holding ready for us."[67] In his poem, "The Past," after agonizing over losses that

---

62. *Letters and Papers*, p. 293.

63. *Letters and Papers*, p. 105.

64. *Letters and Papers*, p. 94.

65. Reported in the historical notes of *Love Letters*, p. 274.

66. *Letters and Papers*, p. 168.

67. *Letters and Papers*, p. 169. He quotes the same text in the sermon for Dietrich Bethge's baptism, p. 295.

elicit "raging defiance" and "besetting anger," the concluding lines run: "The past will come to you once more, and be your life's enduring part, through thanks and repentance."

What are we to make of Bonhoeffer's notion of God seeking again what is past? Is it just religious sentimentality, a kind of baptized wishful thinking? We must admit that the specific connection Dietrich forges with Ecclesiastes 3:15 is unconvincing. This text in context is not about God retrieving our lost happiness, but affirms rather that "what God does lasts forever and nothing can alter it."[68] It does not concern our personal histories, but in fact strikes the pessimistic note that God repeats himself through time, and human beings cannot make things better (cf. 1:9). It is in this sense that he "seeks again what is past."

However, even if given an inadequate exegetical basis in his letters, Bonhoeffer's eschatology is accurate and helpful at this point. Too often when we think of the life to come we mistakenly stress discontinuity with life currently experienced. Heaven is depicted as bodiless existence in clouds with no connection to our lives in this world. Bonhoeffer rightly insists that while God promises us something new, it is a new *creation*, a new *heaven* and a new *earth* that the Bible speaks about. In other words, Christian eschatology is not about bodiless existence but resurrection, not about exchange but radical the transformation of reality.

Bonhoeffer's thought here is comparable to J. R. R. Tolkien's allegorical short story, *Leaf by Niggle*. The painter Niggle spends his life painting leaves that are never quite perfect. Then he dies. In heaven he is found not painting the perfect leaf, but, better still, tending the perfect garden in which are present an abundance of perfect leaves. The message is that what is unfulfilled here, will not be forgotten there, but rather surpassed.

In this light, if *disappointment* concerns the spoiling of this world, eschatology for Bonhoeffer relates to the perfecting or *reappointment* of this world. In response to our disappointments, in an eschatology of reappointment the best things of this world, our relationships of mutual love, will be taken up by the next. In this sense God will indeed restore again what is past. We do well to follow Bonhoeffer's example and give to God those good things that we have lost in order that they might be perfected in glory. Dietrich wrote similarly to Maria: "We must continually bathe all

68. Tremper Longman, *The Book of Ecclesiastes* (NICOT; Grand Rapids: Eerdmans, 1998), p. 124.

that is past in a solution of gratitude and penitence; then we shall gain and preserve it."[69]

7. Remain Cheerful — Spread Hilaritas

With Eberhard Bethge on active military duty in Italy, one of Bonhoeffer's favorite places, Dietrich gave him this advice: "Keep well, enjoy the beautiful country, spread *hilaritas* around you, and keep it to yourself too!"[70] He also wrote to Maria: "Go on being *cheerful,* patient and brave."[71] Cheerfulness was in fact an abiding quality of Dietrich even in the horrors of prison and eventually on death row. His visitors and even the guards were inevitably impressed by it. In his famous poem, "Who Am I?,"[72] the opening stanza reads:

> Who am I? They often tell me
> I would step from my cell's confinement
> calmly, *cheerfully,* firmly, like a squire from his country-house.

Cheerfulness was also something Bonhoeffer appreciated more generally. Commenting on some books he had recently read, Dietrich lamented: "all the newest productions seem to me to lacking in the *hilaritas* — 'cheerfulness' — which is to be found in any really great and free intellectual achievement."[73] In his view, "[a]bsolute seriousness is never without a dash of humour."[74] He wrote approvingly of a colleague that "he has surely kept his *hilaritas.*"[75]

Obviously, *Letters and Papers from Prison* is no "comedy hour." Even so, glimpses of humor do break through, and Dietrich's cheerfulness is in evidence even amidst atrocious conditions. He quips: "Prison life brings home to one how nature carries on uninterruptedly its quiet, open life, and it gives one quite a special — perhaps a sentimental — attitude to-

69. *Letters and Papers,* p. 229.
70. *Letters and Papers,* p. 232.
71. *Love Letters,* p. 56.
72. On the last lines of this poem in which Dietrich finds comfort in being known by God, see Brian S. Rosner, "Known by God: C. S. Lewis and Dietrich Bonhoeffer," *Evangelical Quarterly* 87, no. 4 (2005): 343-52.
73. *Letters and Papers,* p. 189.
74. *Letters and Papers,* p. 376.
75. *Letters and Papers,* p. 243.

wards animal and plant life, except that my attitude towards the flies in my cell remains very unsentimental."[76]

His oldest brother, Karl-Friedrich, a professor of physical chemistry at the universities of Leipzig and Göttingen, wrote to him drolly: "I read recently that the offspring of wild animals born in the zoo have a smaller brain than their contemporaries born wild in natural surroundings. An effect of imprisonment which will perhaps interest you — excuse the feeble joke."[77] At another point, with the winter closing in, Karl-Friedrich wrote: "Now that the most beautiful time of the year is almost over and everywhere outside looks grey and gloomy you may perhaps miss your freedom less."[78]

Bonhoeffer and Bethge wrote back and forth over the naming of Bethge's first child. When the name of Dietrich is floated, Dietrich wrote back to the couple amusingly: "You still seem to be thinking of 'Dietrich.' The name is good, the model less so."[79] After little Dietrich was born, the elder Dietrich wrote: "I'm immensely pleased and proud that you've named your first-born after me. The fact that his birthday comes one day before mine means, no doubt, that he will keep his independence vis-à-vis his namesake uncle, and will always be a little ahead of him."[80]

Likewise, along with sometimes-unbearable pathos, Maria's letters are dotted with a charming wit. At one point she observed concerning her gardening: "The potatoes and turnips are bursting in the heat. So am I, thinking of you."[81] And on another occasion: "It's wonderful to think [my letter] was with you so recently. If only I could mail myself to you in the form of a letter."[82] Elsewhere in the correspondence young Maria wonders modestly whether "it's possible for a married couple to complement each other so that one possesses the good qualities and the other the bad ones."[83] With respect to her own family she wrote: "The Wedemeyers are really

---

76. *Letters and Papers*, p. 71.
77. *Letters and Papers*, p. 98.
78. *Letters and Papers*, p. 103.
79. *Letters and Papers*, p. 177.
80. *Letters and Papers*, p. 208. By way of explanation, Bonhoeffer was Renate Bethge's uncle.
81. *Love Letters*, p. 59.
82. *Love Letters*, p. 62.
83. *Love Letters*, p. 125.

very nice, you know. Belonging to the family is fine, but personally I wouldn't marry into it."[84]

In Dietrich's case cheerfulness was no accident of temperament. Nor was it a lame way of avoiding reality. Rather, it was born of unshakable confidence in God. Humor was one way in which he expressed his trust and assurance in God regardless of the circumstances or the outcome of his strivings: "I'm traveling with gratitude and *cheerfulness* along the road where I'm being led. My past life is brim-full of God's goodness, and my sins are covered by the forgiving love of Christ crucified."[85] The key to cheerfulness in the face of grave disappointment is to know that you are being led, not by the whims, malevolent or otherwise, of men or fate, but by your gracious Heavenly Father who works all things together for your good. It is to be convinced that you know God and are known by him. That Dietrich's cruel incarceration shook him to the core is no surprise. However, as his famous poem, "Who Am I?," demonstrates, what kept Bonhoeffer stable was his belief that his personal identity was not tied to these deprivations. The poem closes with the words:

Who am I? Lonely questions mock me.
Who I really am, you know me, I am yours, O God!

8. Walk Through It with God

How then was Dietrich Bonhoeffer able to endure the ordeal of his incarceration and his impending execution with its crushing disappointments so impressively? Surely it was his unflinching trust in the goodness and sovereignty of God, the God he knew as father, and who knew him as his child.

Bonhoeffer's sense of living life before God can be heard in the Hugo Wolf song he quoted in two letters, to his parents and to Hans von Dohnanyi, his brother-in-law and fellow conspirator: "Over night, over night, come joy and sorrow, and before you know it, both leave you and go to the Lord, to say how you have borne them." According to Dietrich, "it all turns on that 'how,' which is more important than anything that happens to you from the outside."[86]

84. *Love Letters*, p. 238.
85. *Letters and Papers*, p. 393.
86. *Letters and Papers*, pp. 31, 32.

Bonhoeffer was convinced, despite his heartbreaking setbacks, that "such things come from God and from him alone,"[87] In relation to his fiancée's well-being, Dietrich was encouraged that Maria, too, had "learnt very early to recognize a stronger and more gracious hand in what men inflict upon us."[88] He wrote to Maria concerning the German poet Adalbert Stifter's description of pain as "the holiest angel," that "there is an even holier angel than pain, and that is joy in God."[89] He encouraged her to believe that "God is forever upsetting our plans, but only in order to fulfill his own, better plans through us."[90] To Maria's mother he wrote: "We want to receive what God bestows on us with open, outstretched hands and delight in it with all our heart, and with a quiet heart we will sacrifice what God does not yet grant us or takes away from us."[91] Dietrich asks all those experiencing disappointment whether they have sacrificed to God what he has not yet granted. This God-centered view of life's unfulfilled desires is the bedrock of his resilience.

As observers we may understandably be appalled at the apparent futility of Bonhoeffer's tragic story. If so, we need to hear Dietrich's own interpretation of his plight: "I believe that nothing that happens to me is meaningless, and that it is good for us all that it should be so, even if it runs counter to our wishes. As I see it, I'm here for some real purpose, and I only hope to fulfill it. In the light of the great purpose all our privations and disappointments are trivial."[92]

At one point Bonhoeffer actually had an opportunity to escape, but he drew back for fear of endangering his friends still in custody. The following stanza from his poem, "Stations on the Road to Freedom," alludes to this incident and tells how he coped with the disappointment:

Suffering

A change has come indeed. Your hands, so strong and active,
are bound; in helplessness now you see your action
is ended; you sigh in relief, your cause committing

---

87. *Letters and Papers*, p. 32.
88. *Letters and Papers*, p. 180.
89. *Love Letters*, p. 118.
90. *Love Letters*, p. 221.
91. *Letters and Papers*, p. 247.
92. *Letters and Papers*, p. 289.

to stronger hands; so now you may rest contented.
Only for one blissful moment could you draw near to touch freedom;
then, that it might be perfected in glory, you gave it to God.[93]

Bonhoeffer dealt with the agony of the disappointment of having his "*strong and active hands* bound in helplessness" by "committing his cause to *stronger hands.*" Without in any way playing down the joy of a potential escape, the "bliss" of "touching freedom," as he puts it, Bonhoeffer explains that he can willingly forgo it by giving it "to God." The life and thought of Dietrich Bonhoeffer forces us to ask ourselves, have we given our biggest disappointments to God that they might be perfected in glory?

The Consolations of Theology

In order to cope with setbacks and maintain hope Bonhoeffer warns us of the false comforts of wallowing in regret, curbing desire, seeking a substitute, and merely hoping for the resurrection from the dead. Instead, he counsels: (1) Focus on the invaluable; (2) Don't give up on your legitimate desires; (3) Embrace a godly optimism; (4) Don't pretend or minimize the failure; (5) Compare yourself with those less fortunate rather than more fortunate; (6) Find comfort in the God who "seeks again what is past"; (7) Remain cheerful; and above all (8) Give your disappointments to God.

Much of the impact of Bonhoeffer's advice on disappointment is its profound and memorable expression. To recall just a few examples, he believed that "real comfort must break in just as unexpectedly as the distress" and that "God doesn't fill the gap, but keeps it empty." He still believes that "the optimism that is will for the future should never be despised" and that "a mature person's centre of gravity is always where he actually is."

What then is the theology that gave rise to Bonhoeffer's extraordinary life and thought? In one sense it is simply the gospel of the historic Christian faith that he embodied so attractively. In Dietrich's words: "All that we may rightly expect from God, and ask him for, is to be found in Christ Jesus."[94] He believed that the crucifixion of God's Son secured for those who trust in him forgiveness of sins and adoption into God's family. It was this

93. *Letters and Papers,* p. 371.
94. *Letters and Papers,* p. 391.

salvation that gave Dietrich his extraordinary inner strength and purpose. He also believed the cross spelled the end of the world as we know it and that the pernicious powers of this world have already been judged by Christ the Lord and their fate is sealed. Bonhoeffer saw that before the final manifestation of the kingdom of God this crucified Lord "exercises his lordship always and solely through powerlessness, service and the cross."[95] To quote Philippians 4:7, amidst devastating failure, Dietrich Bonhoeffer experienced the "peace of God, which transcends all understanding," a peace that "protected his heart and his mind in Christ Jesus."

Part of Bonhoeffer's contribution to Christian theology is his refusal to allow one truth to obscure another. It is this disavowal of damaging false bifurcations from which many of the lessons for coping with disappointment emerge. He holds things together that others mistakenly assume to be mutually exclusive. He believes in *both* divine sovereignty *and* responsible action, *both* bold deeds *and* gracious forgiveness; *both* caring deeply *and* not despairing, *both* loving this world *and* eagerly anticipating the next. Bonhoeffer knows he is not the author of his own life. Yet that doesn't stop him from dreaming and yearning and hoping and working. The day after the plot to kill Hitler failed, he concluded, "[it is] only by living completely in this world that one learns to have faith."[96]

---

95. Eberhard Bethge, *Dietrich Bonhoeffer: Theologian, Christian, Contemporary* (London: Collins, 1970), p. 769.

96. *Letters and Papers*, p. 369.

C. S. LEWIS
on Pain

ROBERT BANKS

The sufferings of this present time are not worthy to be compared with the glory that is to be revealed in us.

Romans 8:18

Introduction: Pain Described

It was Monday morning, 18 July 1960. Two taxis carried the mourners the short distance from the family home, the Kilns, to the crematorium just outside Oxford. C. S. Lewis, his two young stepsons, David and Douglas, and his brother Warnie were in the first car. The cleaning lady and handyman at the Kilns, and the Master of Magdalen College, Cambridge, where Lewis was professor, were in the second. By chance, the two cars met up with the hearse carrying Joy's body at the entrance to the crematorium. It was a sunny blustery day, with heavy white clouds warning of possible storms. The mourners trouped into the chapel behind the coffin as the celebrant, the theologian Austin Farrer, began to read the Prayer Book service, choking with emotion as he did so. There was no music. At the close of the service the casket silently bore Joy's body away. When Lewis, his stepsons, and brother returned to the Kilns, he knew it would feel empty. But the reality was staggering and his grief overpowering. Though he often gave way to uncontrollable crying, he found it too hard to talk about what he was feeling, especially with his stepchildren. So he resorted to what he always did when under extreme stress. Wrapping himself in his old dressing gown, he sat down at his desk — the desk at which he had written so many of his academic and popular works — picked up an old exercise book, and began to write.

I shall return to what Lewis — or Jack as he was familiarly known — wrote later in this article, but anyone who has experienced the loss of someone close to them can identify with this outpouring of pent-up feelings. We all experience pain, not just in the lesser sense of a temporary hurt, like an ache in our limbs after exercise, but in the more intense lasting experience of suffering, anguish, and adversity.[1] For pain is an unavoidable part of human experience. It can take a wide variety of forms, e.g., physical injury, material want, domestic abuse, romantic breakup, social rejection, or spiritual struggle, to name just a few. It can spring from illness, loneliness, stress, criticism, mobility, retrenchment, separation, breakdown, failure, remorse, divorce, or bereavement. It includes those affected by car accidents or criminal assaults, the chronically or terminally ill, refugees fleeing from persecution, or the victims of earthquakes, tsunamis, and famine. Pause for a moment to consider the presence of pain in your own life. What has caused you the most persistent pain over the years? What was the most painful experience you have encountered? What is creating the most pain for you in your present situation?

Pain is also frequently mentioned in the Bible. The word, together with such related terms as *sadness, weeping, tears, distress, neediness, grief, affliction, oppression, tribulation,* etc., turns up more than 1800 times, about twice a page throughout Scripture. It is a central issue in a number of biblical writings, for example, the Psalms, Lamentations, Habakkuk, and Revelation, as well in the life of significant biblical figures such as Job, Jeremiah, and Paul. Pain is also problematic for large numbers of Christians. In a recent visit to a popular religious bookshop I found no less than five shelves of books dealing with grief and suffering alone. Such books have their value, but only occasionally do they plumb the full depths of people's suffering or the full force of its challenge, especially for belief or trust in God. You also find books on suffering in general bookshops, some drawing on the fruit of their authors' experience, some offering a range of strategies for managing pain, and some holding out the hope of technological discoveries that will minimize its effects. Only

1. C. S. Lewis, *The Problem of Pain* (London: Geoffrey Bles, 1940), p. 78.

rarely do such books raise the larger existential and philosophical issues that acute pain creates.

In keeping with the theme of this book, I will concentrate on Lewis's discussion of human pain, leaving what he says about animal pain to one side. Although reference to pain appears throughout his writings, apart from his autobiography *Surprised by Joy* and his *Collected Letters*, I will draw primarily on his major treatment in *The Problem of Pain* and, as a kind of extended case study, the detailed record of his bereavement in *A Grief Observed*.

Becoming Acquainted with Pain

How much had Lewis himself experienced pain before he began to write seriously about it?

Early Home Life

He describes his early home life in Belfast as one of "general happiness" based on the blessing of "good parents, good food, and a garden to play in."[2] The only exceptions to this were a child's common encounters with illness, headache, and toothache, occasional nightmares, and then separation from his brother when Warnie was sent off to school in England. One day, when he was nine years old, their father, Albert, told them that Flora, their mother, had cancer. There was an operation, an apparent convalescence, a return of the disease, increasing pain, and finally death. As Albert, unable to cope with the loss of his wife, increasingly withdrew from his children, a "paralysing" rift opened up between them.[3] "Everything that had made the house a home had failed us; everything except one another. We drew daily closer together (that was the good result) — two frightened urchins huddled for warmth in a bleak world. With my mother's death, all settled happiness, all that was tranquil and reliable, disappeared from my life. There was to be much fun, many pleasures, many stabs of Joy; but no more of the old security. It was sea and islands now; the great continent

---

2. C. S Lewis, *Surprised by Joy* (London: Geoffrey Bles, 1955), p. 10.
3. *Surprised by Joy*, p. 21.

had sunk like Atlantis."[4] (Lewis drew deeply upon this profound loss when, in *The Magician's Nephew,* he wrote movingly of Digory's expected loss of his mother.) Flora's illness and death were also the occasion of his first significant religious experience. When his mother's condition was diagnosed as hopeless, "I remembered what I had been taught; that prayers offered in faith would be granted. I accordingly set myself to produce by willpower a firm belief that my prayers for her recovery would be successful; and, as I thought, achieved it. When nevertheless she died I shifted my ground and worked myself into a belief that there was to be a miracle." Though this did not take place, Lewis continued to believe in God, partly because "I was used to things not working, and I thought no more about it," and partly because, like so many children at that age, he viewed God more as a "magician" than as a "Saviour or Judge."[5]

Attending School

A second area of life in which Lewis encountered pain was at school. After Flora's death, his father decided that he should go to boarding school in England. He described going to a strange country with a sadistic headmaster, as "a form of intolerable cruelty."[6] When he followed Warnie to another school in Worcestershire, he encountered toiling and bullying as a regular part of life, especially for intellectually and artistically minded students like himself. It was only when, somewhat over-dramatically, he threatened to kill himself if his father didn't take him away that he was transferred to a better school, under W. T. Kirkpatrick, who helped him develop his formidable reasoning and debating skills. Though Lewis does not directly connect his experience of persecution at school with his loss of faith that took place in his mid-teens, it did play into one of its root causes, "a deeply ingrained pessimism,"[7] more intellectual than psychological, that things did not work out as you had hoped.

---

4. *Surprised by Joy,* pp. 20-21.

5. *Surprised by Joy,* p. 22.

6. D. Gresham, *Jack's Life: Memories of C. S. Lewis* (Nashville: Broadman & Holman, 2005), p. 10.

7. *Surprised by Joy,* p. 56.

First World War

In mid-1917 he started at Oxford University, immediately enlisting in the University Officer's Training Corps. There he developed a close friendship with a fellow Irishman, Paddy Moore; each of them swore that if either were killed they would look after the other's dependent family. On Lewis's nineteenth birthday, after only four weeks full-time training, they landed in northern France. Though for a time all was quiet, during the unending shellfire of the major German Offensive in spring of 1918, they were soon involved in day-to-day fighting. Lewis never forgot "the frights, the cold, the smell, the horribly smashed men moving like half-crushed beetles, the sitting or standing corpses, the landscape of sheer earth without a blade of grass."[8] In mid-April, a shell fired from his own lines landed close by. It killed a sergeant directly in front of him and wounded Lewis in three places,[9] two pieces of shrapnel remaining permanently in his chest. Three poems survive from his wartime experiences. In the first, entitled "Apology," he speaks frankly of war as "this present curse" and as "real hell."[10] The second, "Ode for New Year's Day," evokes the horror of war:

> The sky above is sickening, the clouds of God's hate cover it.
> Body and soul shall suffer beyond all word or thought.
> Till the pain and noisy terror that these first years have wrought
> Seem but the soft arising of the prelude of the storm
> That fiercer still and heavier with sharper lightnings fraught
> Shall pour red wrath upon us over a world deform. . . .[11]

Lewis felt that the war represented the "ending of [an] age in which prayer is vain, God is silent and uncaring."[12] The final poem, "Death in Battle," reveals traces of a more religious longing. This is poignantly expressed in the wistful plea of the slain soldier who, recalling the pain, brutality, and cursing around him, cries out: "Open the gates for me" to the "Country of my dreams" in "the garden of God," for only "this would atone!"[13]

8. *Surprised by Joy*, p. 157.

9. C. S. Lewis, *Collected Letters of C. S. Lewis* (San Francisco: Harper, 2000), vol.1, pp. 367-68, 374.

10. C. S. Lewis, *Spirits in Bondage: A Cycle of Lyrics* (London: Macmillan, 1984), p. 12.

11. *Spirits in Bondage*, p. 13.

12. *Spirits in Bondage*, pp. 14-15.

13. *Spirits in Bondage*, pp. 74-75.

Addressing the Issue: *The Problem of Pain*

According to Lewis, pain was much easier to write about than endure. He was, he says, a coward when it came his way. But his early encounters with pain are significant for two reasons. They show that when he took up the challenge to write about it he did not do so as a purely intellectual exercise. They show that he had experienced typical reactions to pain on the part of those without a genuine Christian faith — the response of secondhand childhood belief, of adolescent atheism, and of aggressive adult unbelief. For Lewis himself these eventually turned out to be steps along the way to genuine faith. A decade after the war ended he gave in and admitted the existence of God and, two years later, acknowledged the uniqueness of Christ's death and resurrection. In agreement with Luther, he said, at the heart of this radical turnabout in his life were the experiences of grace, faith, and being chosen.[14]

Approach and Argument

It was not Lewis's idea to write *The Problem of Pain*. He was invited by an editor to write a book for the average thoughtful person that addressed the main objection people have against Christianity. Lewis agreed and began work on it as the Second World War was getting under way. To understand what he was seeking to do in the book, it is important to get certain things clear.

1. He wrote the book primarily for *unbelievers*. His intentions were apologetic rather than pastoral. Though believers having difficulties with the problem of pain can find many things in it that are helpful, even pastoral, these were not his main audience.

2. He insisted that the book was the work of a *layman* in the Anglican Church, not a trained theologian, and should be read as such. We know, however, that he had passed the manuscript to three theologians representing different denominations to ensure he was not making any embarrassing mistakes.

3. He considered his views quite *traditional*. He was simply restating "ancient and orthodox doctrines," and mentions in particular the ap-

14. *The Problem of Pain*, p. viii.

proach of Augustine. He has "tried to assume nothing that is not professed by all believers,"[15] and if readers come across anything different they should put it down to his ignorance.

How do you react when someone raises the problem of pain as an objection to belief in God? How do you begin to answer them? From my observations, most of us slip into a defensive mode and start offering arguments to counter the objection. This is not the way Lewis begins. Instead he tries to get inside the mind and heart of the objector, drawing on his experience as an atheist. He would recall, he says, how cold and dark the immensity of space appeared and my horror at how human beings "cause pain by being born . . . live by inflicting pain, and in pain . . . mostly die."[16] He would share his realization that possessing reason only enables us to inflict pain on others in more ingenious ways and to increase our own suffering by foreseeing our death. He would talk about how he saw history as largely the story of disease, crime, war, and terror, and that whatever improvements have taken place down the centuries in human affairs are more than outweighed by the effects of evil human inventions, which in the end could destroy all human civilization.

In approaching the problem this way Lewis has followed the Pauline injunction to become all things to all people (1 Cor. 9:19). He identifies with the doubters and gets them onside by showing that he understands their case. Then, he says, I would acknowledge that when I shared the time, I didn't see a puzzling weakness in this objection. If this view of life was correct, how could human beings have ever attributed it to the activity of a wise and loving Creator? Adding a further twist to this, he argues that it is only on the assumption of there being a loving and wise God that the problem of pain becomes really acute. If the universe is just the product of chance or impersonal forces, why should we be aggrieved for the amount of evil and pain within it? But when we entertain the idea of a supernatural and awe-inspiring, moral, and righteous God (glimpses of whom he believed were generally revealed to everyone) who also (as is specially revealed to us in the Scriptures) entered into history in Jesus and changed our relationship to God, pain really becomes a profound issue. This means that we should not consider Christianity a system into which we fit the problem of pain; rather, it is Christianity that creates the problem in its most substantial form.

15. *The Problem of Pain*, p. viii.
16. *The Problem of Pain*, p. 2.

The Nature of God

Even after Lewis has moved the discussion in this surprising direction, he does not begin to defend his Christian beliefs against the problem of pain. Instead he invites the objectors to examine their understanding of God. He begins by stating the problem in its simplest form, in so doing echoing the way Lactantius put it 1,500 years earlier. "If God were good, he would wish to make his creatures perfectly happy, and if God were almighty he would be able to do what he wished. But the creatures are not happy. Therefore God lacks either the goodness, or power, or both."[17] To respond to this, says Lewis, we need first look at some erroneous assumptions built into the words "all-powerful" and "good" when ascribed to God.

The *all-powerfulness* of God is often taken to mean that God can do anything. But, says Lewis, he cannot do what is against his nature or choice. For example, even God cannot make 2 + 2 anything other than 4. Having made the world to work in certain consistent ways, like the force of gravity, he does not arbitrarily change these whenever potential harm rears its head. Though this does not rule out what we call miracles, if God kept changing the way things normally operate in the world, it would be impossible for us to rise to genuine challenges or act responsibly. Unfortunately, fashioning such a reliable world opens up the possibility of people hurting each other in various ways. We might be able to conceive of a world in which God would correct every overstepping of safety, abuse of the free will, or risky natural phenomenon through constantly intervening in our affairs. However, divine short-circuiting of all harmful actions and evil intentions would only destroy human responsibility and freedom.

Lewis then examines how people tend to understand the *goodness* of God. If the difference between our human and a divine view of goodness is too great, we would not be able to distinguish God from an evil Fiend. Unless we have some sense of God's standards, Jesus would not have been able to call us to repent from our ways. The trouble is that people frequently water down the meaning of goodness. They do this when they view love as merely showing kindness or as seeking others' happiness. It is because people attach a shallower meaning of love to God that the problem of reconciling human suffering with divine goodness arises. They need to see that for God, love is "pure giving" and that ultimately love is not about others'

17. *The Problem of Pain*, p. 14.

kindness, our happiness, or even our love for God, but about God's love for us as sacrificially demonstrated in Christ.

Our Human Culpability

It is only after clarifying what is meant by God's goodness and power that Lewis begins to provide specific counter-arguments for who is responsible for the problem of pain. His explanation is what in apologetic terms is called the *free-will defense.* What this involves, he says, is a need for recovery by modern people of "the old sense of sin." Sin must be reclaimed from the way in which it has been sentimentalized, psychologized, and statistically relativized in favor of what is allegedly "normal." At the root of this sense of sin is our abuse of free will by disobeying God. This began with the fall, which for Lewis was a historical event passed on by heredity. For him, most of the problem of pain stems from wanting "some corner of the universe in which we could say to God 'This is our business, not yours.'"[18] A direct consequence of our self-centeredness is our causing pain to others. It is not God, but humans, he says, "who have produced racks, whips, prisons, slavery, guns, bayonets, and bombs: it is by human avarice or stupidity, not the churlishness of nature, that we have poverty and overwork."[19] For Lewis, the greatest part of human suffering stems from this source, much of the remainder coming from failing to live responsibly in a divinely created, risk-laden world.

The Purposes of Pain

At this point many Christians would turn from talking about the problem of pain to presenting its gospel answer. Lewis moves in the same direction but in a more integrated way through exploring the positive outcomes of pain.

1. The experience of pain is sometimes required to bring us to the point of realizing *our need for God.* According to one of Lewis's best-known statements about pain, "God whispers to us in our pleasures,

18. *The Problem of Pain,* p. 68.
19. *The Problem of Pain,* p. 77.

speaks in our conscience, but shouts in our pains: it is his megaphone to rouse a deaf world."[20] Through it, says Lewis, God "plants the flag of truth within the fortress of a rebel soul."[21] Pain reminds us that the good things in life, which are finite, and our earthly life itself, which is mortal, cannot give us what we basically desire. Lewis did not believe that pain is God's direct judgment upon people, meted out according to how much they have offended him or others. Often it is something we bring upon ourselves because of our selfish actions, and sometimes it falls more on people who are more decent and caring.

2. As "rebels who must lay down our arms in self-surrender . . . to God,"[22] our *turning to him* involves "a kind of death," and requires us to "die daily" in an ongoing way.[23] A graphic example of the pain involved in this initial act of surrender to God is the portrayal of Eustace's de-dragoning, or conversion, in *The Voyage of the Dawn Treader* (1955).[24]

3. After our conversion, we still operate with so many mixed motives in *pursuing God's will*. Only when our "action is contrary to our inclinations, or (in other words) painful,"[25] can we be more confident that we are doing what God wants. According to Lewis, this principle of new life through death is written into the way the Creation operates (cf. 1 Cor. 15:35-42) but it is most fully expressed in Christ's suffering and death for us on Calvary (Matt. 27:45-46). There, not only "all natural supports, but the presence of the very Father to whom the sacrifice is made deserts and forsakes" him.[26] Since, in essence, what God calls upon us to do has already in some sense been accomplished by Christ, it is a great help to know that "a master's hand is holding ours" as we follow in his steps.[27] In these three ways, says Lewis, realizing our need, turning to God, and pursuing God's will, it is through pain that we come to depend upon the suffering of Christ and are "made perfect through suffering" (Heb. 2:10).

Some make a further objection at this point. While all this may make sense on an individual basis, the overwhelming tragedy of mass suffering

20. *The Problem of Pain*, p. 81.
21. *The Problem of Pain*, p. 83.
22. *The Problem of Pain*, p. 79.
23. *The Problem of Pain*, pp. 79-80.
24. C. S. Lewis, *The Voyage of the Dawn Treader* (London: Bodley Head, 1952), pp. 81-92.
25. *The Problem of Pain*, p. 87.
26. *The Problem of Pain*, pp. 90-91.
27. *The Problem of Pain*, p. 92.

— as during an epidemic, famine, or earthquake — creates an unanswerable challenge to belief in God. Lewis tackles this difficulty in a surprising way. There is "no such thing as a sum of suffering, for no one suffers it. When we have reached the maximum that a single person can suffer, we have, no doubt, reached something very horrible, but we have reached all the suffering there can ever be in the universe. The addition of a million fellow-sufferers adds no more pain."[28] In a sermon Lewis preached during the early years of World War II while writing *A Problem of Pain,* he said: "We think of the streets in Warsaw and confront the deaths there with an abstraction called Life." But ultimately it is only a question of *our* death and *how* it will happen. War does not change the fact that we all die, it only puts some deaths earlier; it does not necessarily make death more painful, sometimes the opposite is the case. What war does, in a way we cannot avoid, is "make death real to us."[29]

An Eternal Perspective

For some, however, this kind of mass suffering is still not the most basic objection to belief in God. What about the everlasting suffering Christianity mandates for those who reject God and are consigned to hell? This *existence of hell,* he says rightly, has the full support of Scripture, particularly of Jesus' own teaching, and of Christian theology down through the centuries. It is also a reasonable and ethical belief. To put it simply, "if a game is to be played, it must be possible to lose it." Since those who choose against God go against his deepest longing that people "freely love him in return,"[30] he will not force them to believe and they in fact would not want this.

- To those who object that the reality of hell is contrary to belief in a loving God, he answers that God simply gives people what they wish, that is, to be fully separate from him. The alternatives — to condone what they choose or forgive if they do not change — would entail

28. *The Problem of Pain,* pp. 103-4.
29. C. S. Lewis, "Learning in War Time," *Fernseeds and Elephants and Other Essays on Christianity* (London: Collins, 1970), pp. 26-38.
30. *The Problem of Pain,* p. 108.

treating their choice as good or permitting them to operate in heaven in a self-centered way.

- To those who object to the disproportionate length and intensity of pains in hell portrayed in some passages of Scripture, he responds that Jesus' language of eternal punishment, banishment into darkness, and torment by fire, are all images that speak of final separation rather than timelessness. In any case, it is only the "remains" of a real person — the kind of shadowy, wraithlike ghost he imaginatively pictures in his book *The Great Divorce* (1946) — that survive.
- To those who object that it is hard to see how believers could be happy in heaven knowing that some were in hell, he suggests that we should not think of hell as parallel to heaven so much as the darkness outside, "the outer rim where being fades away into nonentity."[31]

Lewis concludes that "in the long run the answer to all those who object to the doctrine of hell, is itself a question: 'What are you asking God to do?' To wipe out their past sins and, at all costs, to give them a fresh start, smoothing every difficulty and offering every miraculous help? But he has done so, on Calvary. To forgive them? They will not be forgiven. To leave them alone? Alas, I am afraid that is what He does."[32]

To properly understand pain we must, says Lewis, view it from the *perspective of heaven*. Failing to do this, he says, would be like "leaving out almost one side of the account."[33] He takes as his leitmotiv here Paul's declaration that "the sufferings of this present time are not worthy to be compared with the glory that is to be revealed in us" (Rom. 8:18): Far from being an exercise in escapism or a form of spiritual bribery, heaven is the ultimate reality that people unconsciously long for in their earthly search for happiness and security. This is why nothing in this world — even such wonderful divine gifts as books, hobbies, landscapes, friends, spouses — fail to fully satisfy us. "Our Father refreshes us on the journey with some pleasant inns, but will not encourage us to mistake them for home."[34] Through an array of evocative images and tender appeals Lewis seeks to direct his readers to the God for whom they were made and in whom they

---

31. *The Problem of Pain*, p. 115.
32. *The Problem of Pain*, p. 116.
33. *The Problem of Pain*, p. 132.
34. *The Problem of Pain*, p. 103.

will alone find their destiny. Everyday life is full of clues to his presence, if only people would open their eyes and yield themselves to him. Self-giving, the very opposite of that which causes the majority of suffering in both this world and the next, is rooted in the heart of God, and is perfectly expressed in Christ's sacrifice on Calvary and his eternal relationship with the Father. Life in the new world God is creating will take the form of a divine dance whose steps and movements are swept along purely by God's self-giving or love.

Reactions and Evaluation

Reactions to *The Problem of Pain* varied. One reviewer at the time wittily remarked that the problem of pain was bad enough without Mr. Lewis's adding to it by writing a book on the subject! Lewis's close friend, the author Charles Williams, commented wryly that the weight of God's displeasure was reserved for Job's comforters, "the sort of people" he said, "who wrote books on the problem of pain."[35] More seriously, though not persuaded by Lewis's views on animal pain, the philosopher C. E. M. Joad regarded Lewis's book as the most elaborate and careful account on the subject and was helped by it to overcome the main hurdle that had prevented him from coming to faith.[36] Peter Schakel, though he finds as yet few of "the analogies which later became almost the defining characteristic of his apologetic style,"[37] nevertheless genuinely admired the work. An atheist philosopher, Antony Flew, criticized the book's reliance on the "free will defence,"[38] arguing that God could have arranged all the laws of nature so that people would always freely choose what is right. However, another philosopher, Basil Mitchell, rejoined that Flew's view rests on his conviction that belief in God is illogical.[39] Interestingly, in recent years Flew him-

35. C. S. Lewis & others, *Essays Presented to Charles Williams* (Oxford: Oxford University Press, 1966), p. xiii.
36. C. E. M. Joad, *The Recovery of Belief: A Restatement of Christian Philosophy* (London: Faber, 1952).
37. Peter Schakel, *Reason and Imagination in C. S. Lewis: A Study of Till We Have Faces* (Grand Rapids: Eerdmans, 1984), p. 171.
38. A. Flew, "Divine Omnipotence and Human Freedom," *New Essays in Philosophical Theology*, ed. A. Flew and A. MacIntyre (London: SCM, 1955), pp. 144-69.
39. Basil Mitchell, *The Justification of Religious Belief* (London: Macmillan, 1973), p. 10.

self has changed his mind and accepted that belief in God is after all philosophically defensible.

A more extended critique of *The Problem of Pain* comes from another philosopher. In his book *C. S. Lewis and the Search for Rational Religion* (1985), John Beversluis argues that since, for Lewis, pain is God's megaphone, one could infer that the less or more a person suffers the closer or further they must be from God. But this is not a necessary inference from what Lewis said. He also argues that even if hardened sinners did repent and turn to God it would not be freely chosen but rather would be like a forced confession from a captured prisoner. This overlooks the way God operates from love, not coercion. In any case, as Alan Jacobs has recently pointed out, even in *The Problem of Pain* Lewis does not just build a case through reasoned arguments. Through picturesque metaphors, striking analogies, and familiar illustrations, he presents a Christian vision of reality, one that is inextricably linked to the overarching biblical story of Creation, Fall, Redemption, Sanctification, Judgment, and Re-Creation. Just as Lewis's own conversion came about not only through arguments but through being grasped by the reality of Christ's death and resurrection and by the centrality of Christ within the wider story of God's purpose for his creation, so here as well.[40] Beversluis entirely misses this appeal to the imagination as well as reason, as if he were listening to Lewis monaurally rather than stereophonically.

There are, I suggest, three minor criticisms that can be made of *The Problem of Pain*. First, Lewis does not give enough attention to the residue of randomness and disastrous accident in the world, through earthquakes, hurricanes, floods, and the like, that cannot wholly be turned into something purposeful. While one may argue that much of the suffering they cause is due to people ignoring past occurrences and continuing to live in high-risk places, Lewis might, as he did with some animal pain, explore further the role of Satan in fracturing the created order. In my experience with the Agnostic Anonymous groups that I ran over many years, what people present as an intellectual problem with pain mostly has its basis in an experience of loss or suffering, often as a child, affecting someone close to them. Unless the problem is dealt with at this level, in part through the

---

40. See J. Beversluis, *C. S. Lewis and the Search for Rational Religion* (Grand Rapids: Eerdmans, 1985), pp. 101-20 and A. Jacobs, *The Narnian: The Life & Imagination of C. S. Lewis* (San Francisco: Harper, 2005), p. 238.

stories of others who found a way through it, it will not be resolved by rational argument. Second, though Lewis talks about Christ's redemptive sacrifice for us and of his self-sacrificial life as a model for our imitation, as Alister McGrath says, he could have emphasized more the fact that since God suffered in Christ, "He knows what it is like to experience pain . . . abandonment, suffering and death."[41] However, Lewis here is expounding a theodicy, or defense of belief in God against specific objections, not a theology of the relationship between Father and Son, and no full-scale treatment of this subject is required in our apologetics and evangelism.

Deepening Encounters with Pain

During the next two decades of his life, Lewis had several further encounters with pain.

Public Opposition

The first came from opposition to his public Christian stand. In English universities, at the time, Christianity was not only held in disrepute but disdain. Although Lewis was becoming very highly regarded for his work on medieval literature, especially his magisterial *Allegory of Love* (1936), his apologetic writing and broadcasting placed a question mark against his academic reputation. The words underneath the picture of Lewis on the cover of *Time* magazine in 1947, "His Heresy: Christianity," perfectly describe what he was up against. As his biographer Alan Jacobs notes, "It began to be said that Lewis was wasting his time on cheap popular sermonizing and science fiction, time that would have been better spent on his scholarship."[43] This was the basic reason for Lewis's being overlooked for both the Merton Chair of English Literature in 1947 and the Professorship in Poetry in 1952 at Oxford when he was clearly the best candidate. His reputation suffered a further setback when he began to write children's sto-

---

41. A. McGrath, *Bridge-Building: Effective Christian Apologetics* (London: Hodder & Stoughton, 1993), pp. 144ff. and, more extensively, in his book *Suffering* (London: Hodder & Stoughton, 1992).

42. C. S. Lewis, *The Four Loves* (London: Geoffrey Bles, 1960).

43. Jacobs, *The Narnian*, p. 264.

ries. Though it was acceptable for an Oxford scholar to write detective stories in his spare time — on the basis that "all dons at some time get sick and have to read something in bed," writing for children was way out of bounds. Lewis was dispirited and wounded at this unfair and discriminatory treatment by his peers. It was only when the rival Cambridge University set up a new Chair in Medieval and Renaissance Literature especially with Lewis in mind, that he received appropriate recognition.

Deteriorating Health

A second way in which pain came Lewis's way was through his deteriorating health. The small illnesses he had suffered as a child continued into middle age.[44] In many ways his whole life was "a succession of colds, toothaches . . . and flu."[45] This flow of ordinary aches and pains occasionally had its humorous side. When some years later he was suffering from mumps, Lewis reported to another friend that his doctor H. E. Havard (a member of the Inklings who wrote a medical appendix to *The Problem of Pain*) "kept quoting me bits out of the book, which I thought was a bit thick."[46] Like so many returned soldiers, he suffered from a recurrent nightmare and headaches. In mid-1949, just after he'd finished writing the first of his Narnia Chronicles, he had a physical breakdown, collapsed, and was hospitalized. Much of this was due to how much time and effort he had to put into looking after an increasingly demanding Mrs. Moore, a situation that worsened when he had to care for Warnie during the latter's intermittent alcoholic binges. Consequently Lewis did not look after himself properly, eating unhealthily and exercising less. From his late fifties, his heart began to wear out. He was also suffering from an enlarged prostate and kidney problems that required him to wear a catheter. During the last years of his life, his body was more that of a man in his mid-seventies than early sixties.

---

44. Lewis, *Collected Letters*, vol. 1, p. 877.

45. K. Lindskoog, *Mere Christian* (Downers Grove, Ill.: InterVarsity Press, 1981), p. 130.

46. See further R. E. Havard, "Philia: Jack at Ease," *C. S. Lewis at the Breakfast Table and Other Reminiscences*, ed. J. T. Como (New York: Harcourt & Brace, 1992), pp. 215-28.

Joy's Death

The last way in which pain came to him was through Joy's battle with, temporary remission from, and eventual death through cancer. Interestingly, two years before Joy's diagnosis with cancer, the wife of one of his regular overseas correspondents became gravely and then terminally ill. Lewis continued to write often, helping his friend to cope with and understand his wife's death. Their story and Lewis's letters were later included in the book by Sheldon Vanauken, *A Severe Mercy*.[47] In hindsight we can see how Lewis's role here provided a kind of rehearsal for what Joy was to face, and the letters he wrote form a kind of halfway house between the argumentative approach in *The Problem of Pain* and the confessional character of what he wrote after Joy's death. When she was recovering from her first bout with cancer, Lewis had a strange experience. As Joy's pain was decreasing in proportion to the rise in calcium levels in her legs, he suffered a loss of calcium and a growing pain in his own legs. He believed he had been allowed by God to accept Joy's pain to relieve hers.

Enduring the Reality: *A Grief Observed*

When he began writing about his grief, Lewis decided to use only what he had at hand, filling up four notebooks he found lying in his desk. He started about two weeks after Joy's death and stopped just over a month later. He wrote, he said, about himself, his dead wife, and God "in that order," creating a kind of "map of sorrow" as "a safety valve" to prevent a "total collapse."[48] Over the last few decades, studies of reactions to grief, though over a longer period of time, have been analyzed by the likes of Kübler-Ross, the Australians M. and D. McKissock, and John Bowlby. The theologian Ann Loades points out that *A Grief Observed* includes reference to Kübler-Ross's categories — denial, anger, bargaining, depression, and acceptance — though not necessarily in that order.[49] The McKissocks' more flexible approach — fea-

---

47. See S. Vanauken, *A Severe Mercy* (New York: Harper & Row, 1977). There were eight letters about the illness and death his friend's wife and later six about Joy's illness and death.

48. C. S. Lewis, *A Grief Observed* (London: Faber, 1961), pp. 47, 49.

49. See A. Loades, "C. S. Lewis: Grief Observed, Rationality Abandoned, Faith Regained," *Journal of Literature and Theology* 3, no. 4 (1989); E. Kübler-Ross, *On Death & Dying* (New York: Scribner's, 1970).

turing anger, guilt, despair, depression, and replacement[50] — and especially
John Bowlby's four-stage model — numbness and angry or distressful out-
bursts, yearning and searching for the lost figure, disorganization and despair, a growing degree of order and structure — come closer.[51]

Approach and Argument

Shock and numbness: Lewis begins by revealing his feelings of fear, un-
ease, restlessness, loneliness, and disorientation in the wake of Joy's death.
He also notes the lack of energy, indeed laziness, that grief induces. Also
how little he felt able to talk to his two stepsons or acquaintances because
of the embarrassment it produced. Some countervailing feelings also sur-
faced, e.g., "love is not the whole of a man's life," "I was happy before I ever
met her," "I've plenty of what people call resources," and "people get over
these things." But then there would come "a sudden jab of red-hot memory and all this 'common-sense' vanishes" in an outpouring of "tears and
pathos." Yet this, too, can all easily veer into something maudlin, self-
pitying, and indulgent.[52]

Joy's death also unleashed deep feelings from his childhood that he
had never fully worked through. "Cancer, and cancer, and cancer. My
mother, my father, my wife. I wonder who is next in the queue?"[53] Regarding Joy herself, though Lewis was afraid of going to places associated with
her he determined to do so. But it was there he felt her absence most
keenly. Where he felt her presence most was in his own body, which "had
feasted on love; every mode of it" so that "no cranny . . . remained unsatis-
fied."[54] To his dismay he found he did not have even one good photograph
of her and that, though her voice was still vivid, he could no longer imagine her face distinctly.

What about God? All his efforts at praying seemed to result in having
"a door slammed in your face, and a sound of bolting and double bolting
on the inside and, after that, silence." Why, he asks, despite what is usually

50. M. & D. McKissock, *Coping with Grief,* 3rd ed. (Sydney: ABC, 1995).

51. J. Bowlby, "Processes of Mourning," *International Journal of Psycho-Analysis* 42 (1961): 317-40.

52. *A Grief Observed,* pp. 7-8.

53. *A Grief Observed,* p. 12.

54. *A Grief Observed,* p. 13.

said, does God appear "so very absent in a time of trouble"?[55] Does being reminded that Christ himself felt abandoned on the cross make it easier to understand a God who seems like a Silent Jailer? After all, Christ was the One on whom "the torments of hope — of suspense, of anxiety — were at the last moment loosed."[56] For the time being Lewis had no answer. For all this, he did not feel in any danger of losing faith in God, only that in some way God was different to what he had previously believed.

Longing and protest: Lewis began his second notebook by commenting on how appalled he was at reading over the contents of the first one. It showed him how much he was more preoccupied with *his* loss of Joy than with what her death had cost *her*. He mentions how he had responded to some typical reactions to her death. To ordinary unbelievers who tried to comfort him by saying "she will live forever in my memory," he exclaims "Live? That's exactly what she won't do," and for her to be nothing more than an image in his memory is to verge on a kind of idolatry. On the other hand, most of his academic colleagues didn't think she continued to exist in any sense all. To them he declares his belief in her ongoing life in a new kind of body and space-time environment. His fellow Christians sought to encourage him by affirming "she is with God," but since "the thing I really want — the jokes, the drinks, the arguments, the lovemaking, the tiny heartbreaking . . . commonplace is impossible," this didn't lessen his grief.[57] To such people he wanted to say bluntly: "Talk to me about the truth of religion, and I'll listen gladly. Talk to me about the duty of religion and I'll listen submissively. But don't come to me talking about the consolations of religion or I shall suspect that you don't understand." For "all that stuff about family reunions 'on the further shore,' pictured in entirely earthly terms . . . is . . . all out of bad hymns . . . There's not a word about it in the Bible."[58]

This leads him to question the central position he had advocated in *The Problem of Pain*. In Freudian fashion he asks, "What reason have we, except our own desperate wishes, to believe that God is, by any standard we can conceive, 'good'? Doesn't all the prima facie evidence suggest exactly the opposite?"[59] For "in the only life we know he hurts us beyond our worst

---

55. *A Grief Observed*, p. 9.
56. C. S. Lewis, *Letters to Malcolm, Chiefly on Prayer* (London: Geoffrey Bles, 1964), p. 62.
57. *A Grief Observed*, p. 22.
58. *A Grief Observed*, p. 23.
59. *A Grief Observed*, p. 26.

fears and beyond all we can imagine."[60] He remembers all the prayers he and Joy had offered, the hope that came not just from their longings but from scientific X-rays, surprising remissions, and a miraculous recovery. "Step by step we were 'led up the garden path,'" and "Time after time, when God seemed most gracious, he was really preparing the next torture."[61] Perhaps we are just "rats in a laboratory" at the hands of a vivisecting God?[62] While we can call on Christ to answer this, what about his last words on the cross that God had also forsaken him (Matt. 27:45-47)?

Looking back over these remarks the next day, Lewis described what he had written as "a yell rather than a thought" and that he needed to go over the same ground again. He starts by asking, "Is it rational to believe in a . . . Cosmic Sadist?"[63] But until he can give more attention to this, he just has to get on with the fact that for him, "the starboard engine has gone" and "I, the port engine, must chug along somehow till we make a harbour, or rather, till the journey ends."[64] This was the case with his mother's death when he was nine, and it is now the case with Joy's.

Assessment and reframing: Lewis begins his third notebook by saying that his most painful moments come precisely when he is not thinking of Joy. In part this was due to a continual vague sense of "something amiss."[65] He realizes that he has to balance his feeling with more thinking. For example, did her death introduce any new factor that could affect his belief in God? As a follower of Christ he already knew he could not expect worldly happiness and that suffering was part of the deal. "We were told 'Blessed are they that mourn' and I accepted it." Yet "it is different when the thing happens to oneself, not to others, and in reality, not in imagination. . . . If I had really cared, as I thought I did, about the sorrows of the world, I should not have been so overwhelmed when my own sorrow came. It has been an imaginary faith playing with counters labelled 'Illness,' 'Pain,' 'Death' and 'Loneliness.'" You do not discover "how serious your faith is . . . until you are not playing for counters . . . but for every penny you have in the world. Nothing less will shake a man like me out of his merely verbal thinking."[66]

60. *A Grief Observed*, p. 25.
61. *A Grief Observed*, p. 27.
62. *A Grief Observed*, p. 26.
63. *A Grief Observed*, p. 27.
64. *A Grief Observed*, p. 29.
65. *A Grief Observed*, p. 30.
66. *A Grief Observed*, pp. 31-32.

Yet, as far as it went, his faith prior to Joy's death was real, and it was becoming even more real now. To call God a "Cosmic Sadist," therefore, sprang more from anguish than understanding. It would be more accurate to see God as a kind of "Cosmic Surgeon,"[67] whose intentions are wholly good. The trouble is that "the kinder and more conscientious he is, the more he will go on cutting. If he yielded to your entreaties, if he stopped before the operation was complete, all the pain up to that point would have been useless." Just as Jesus had to endure pain to the full (something Lewis had graphically portrayed in his description of Aslan's death in *The Lion, the Witch and the Wardrobe*), so must we when it comes our way.[68] Then unexpectedly one morning Lewis wakes to find that his heart is lighter than it has been for weeks, and puts this down to a sounder night's sleep, the sun reappearing after ten cloudy days, and a memory of Joy when he was least thinking of her. The removal of this barrier makes him realize that "you can't see anything properly while your eyes are blurred with tears."[69] He finds the same happening more with God. "I have gradually been coming to feel that the door is no longer shut and bolted. Was it my own frantic need that slammed it in my face?"[70] Did not Jesus say that it is only when we are ready to knock that the door will be opened, and only when we are ready to receive that "it shall be given" (Matt. 13:12)?[71]

Lewis now begins to view his relationship with Joy like a dance frozen in mid-step that is beginning a new movement. This helps him get beyond worrying about how imaginary or real is his memory of Joy, and he begins to find her presence everywhere, not as a strong feeling or a kind of vision but as a pervasive reality. He also sees that God was not trying to test his faith, for "he always knew my temple was a house of cards" and "the only way of making me realize the fact was to knock it down."[72] As his faith begins to strengthen, he feels it's like having a leg amputated and being replaced with a pair of crutches. But just as he thinks he is making progress, "Tonight all the hells of young grief have opened again; the mad words, the bitter resentment, the fluttering in the stomach, the nightmare unreality, the wallowed-in tears. For in grief nothing 'stays put.' One keeps on emerg-

67. *A Grief Observed*, pp. 33-34.
68. *A Grief Observed*, pp. 36-37.
69. *A Grief Observed*, p. 37.
70. *A Grief Observed*, p. 38.
71. *A Grief Observed*, p. 38.
72. *A Grief Observed*, pp. 42-43.

ing from a phase, but it always recurs. Round and round. Everything repeats . . . the same leg is cut off time after time. The first plunge of the knife
into the flesh is felt again and again."[73] So ends the third notebook.

Surrender and acceptance: In the final one Lewis continues this
theme. "I was wrong," says Lewis, "to say that the stump was recovering
from the pain of amputation. I was deceived because it has so many ways
to hurt me that I discover them one by one."[74] Yet there is progress. This
has not come as "a sudden, striking, and emotional transition" but more
like "the warming of a room or the coming of daylight" that unknowingly
has been approaching for some time.[75] Lewis realizes, however, that up to
this point he has focused most on himself, next on his wife, and only then
on God, when it would have been better to reverse the order. This is the
way not only to "enjoy Him" but also to "enjoy Joy" more.[76] As he begins to
do so, he finds images, rather than memories, of her coming to him. One is
of her as a garden being cultivated through their time together, to prepare
her for her new life. Another is of her as a sword, being grasped by God,
weighing it and slicing the air and declaring it "a right Jerusalem blade."[77]
He finds this gives an altogether new meaning to the phrase "She is in
God's hands" that had meant so little to him before.

Though Lewis doesn't take this experience as proof of anything, and is
aware how easily we can turn our images into idols, he realizes afresh that
till now his "incurably abstract intellect" and his numerous "assumptions"
have let through just a small amount of "total reality."[78] He needs God,
"the Great Iconoclast," to continue shattering his neat little categories and
preconceptions. "The trouble is that it is so easy to have others, as well as
our Saviour and the Father neatly taped and boxed. What we need is not
our idea of these but the other, Christ and God themselves, and we can
only find the first through the second."[79] Now, just as while Joy was alive
his task had been to put God first, so he must do in her absence. "I know
the two great commandments, and I'd better get on with them," he says,

73. *A Grief Observed*, p. 46.
74. *A Grief Observed*, p. 48.
75. *A Grief Observed*, p. 49.
76. *A Grief Observed*, p. 49.
77. *A Grief Observed*, p. 50.
78. *A Grief Observed*, p. 51.
79. *A Grief Observed*, p. 56.

leaving behind questions and problems that God "did not set me at all" and to which there is no need to know the answer.[80]

The following evening he had a new kind of experience of Joy's presence. "It was quite incredibly unemotional. Just the impression of her mind momentarily facing my own . . . not at all like a rapturous reunion of lovers. More like getting a telephone call or a wire from her about a practical arrangement" in which there was ". . . an extreme and cheerful intimacy."[81] This makes him wonder afresh what our resurrected life with those close to us on earth will be like. As yet we cannot fully know and, because the truth will be so much greater than we can conceive, perhaps we should simply leave it at that. His closing image is of the beautiful smile on Joy's face when she died that, initially, he assumed was directed to him but thinking back now realizes was directed to God into whose loving and welcoming presence she was about to enter. At that point Lewis stopped writing and laid down his pen.

Reactions and Evaluation

Lewis had no intention of publishing this account of his grief. It was only at the urging of his young friend Roger Lancelyn Green, who felt that many people would be helped by it, that he ultimately did so, and even then hiding his identity under a pseudonym. This strategy was so successful that, ironically, when the book appeared several of his friends sent him copies suggesting "you might find this helpful"! I have to say that, despite the different circumstances of my own bereavement — not just four but more than thirty years of marriage, not an ongoing inner turmoil during bereavement but an ongoing sense of God's considerateness — of all the books I read at that time *A Grief Observed* proved to be by far the most helpful.

From the start the book was acknowledged for its piercing honesty and graphic prose, and for nearly fifty years it has been a spiritual companion to people in mourning. For all that, it has not been without its detractors. One critic called it a case of "sheer exhibitionism," somewhat unfair in the light of Lewis's reluctance and discretion in putting it out. Another

80. *A Grief Observed*, pp. 55-56.
81. *A Grief Observed*, pp. 58-59.

objected to its maudlin elements, failing to notice Lewis's frequent self-criticisms of this tendency. Lewis's friend Austin Farrer, who was writing a book on suffering at the time,[82] felt that some of the arguments in *The Problem of Pain* were too abstract to console Lewis himself, forcing him toward a more existential solution.[83] The feature film *Shadowlands* similarly depicts Lewis's holding on to faith as the result of a leap of faith more than biblical assurance. This sounds more like the way some people have interpreted Kierkegaard, a writer Lewis considered possibly helpful to others but did not find helpful himself. Ann Loades concurs, arguing that "Lewis has now caved in intellectually."[84] She points to the conclusion of his book *Till We Have Faces,* and reference to Christ's "union of total privation with total adherence to God," in discussing Psalm 22 in his *Reflections on the Psalms,*[85] suggesting that Lewis finally gave himself up to God's silent *absence* rather than presence. Such a view overlooks the positive element in his comments, toward the end of *A Grief Observed,* about the beginning of his rediscovery of joy in learning to praise God,[86] and seeing everything from God's perspective again.[87]

John Beversluis, whose critique of *The Problem of Pain* has already been mentioned, disagrees with this, arguing that for all the book's emotional content, it is "a rational attempt to grasp the implications of suffering." For "by giving his emotions their head and allowing himself to experience their full impact . . . he could better comprehend and come to terms with his loss."[88] We could say, then, that *A Grief Observed* is Lewis's equivalent of the Book of Job. In it he "grieves like a husband but thinks like an apologist."[89] According to Beversluis, the real difficulty with the book is Lewis's now giving up altogether the belief that God's notion of goodness has anything at all to do with ours. He argues that Lewis has moved to a purely fideistic viewpoint, believing in God in spite of rather than because of rational evidence. This is contradicted by a letter Bever-

82. A. Farrer, *Love Almighty and Ills Unlimited* (London: Clarendon, 1962).

83. A. Farrer, "The Christian Apologist," *Light on C. S. Lewis,* ed. J. Gibb (London: Geoffrey Bles, 1965), pp. 23-43.

84. Loades, "C. S. Lewis," 117.

85. C. S. Lewis, *Reflections on the Psalms* (London: Geoffrey Bles, 1958), p. 106.

86. *A Grief Observed,* p. 53.

87. *A Grief Observed,* pp. 60-61.

88. Beversluis, *Search for Rational Religion,* pp. 141-42.

89. Beversluis, *Search for Rational Religion,* p. 46.

sluis himself received from Lewis around this time,[90] which shows, as Victor Reppert argues, how much Lewis had reaffirmed and deepened the arguments in *The Problem of Pain* through the crucible of suffering.[91] His difficulty with Joy's death arose more basically from his not having "the firm trust in God's wisdom that he thought he had."[92] While, no more than Job, does he receive answers to all his questions, what he gets is a deeper understanding of God, surrendering to which puts his loss of Joy in a larger perspective.

Conclusion: Pain Transcended

In many ways *A Grief Observed* provides a model of how we ought to grieve, and help people who grieve after a serious, unexpected loss. Not just the grief that attends bereavement but any form of grief, such as the sudden loss of a job, marriage, health, reputation, or success. While Lewis said during his experience of loss he did not want anyone to offer him simplistic pious consolations, his book does offer some genuine consolations arising from its lived theology of suffering. At a basic level, Lewis's account reminds us of the following — that coping with pain is sometimes affected by such circumstantial factors as how much sleep we get, what the weather is like, and whether our memories are positive ones; that the experience among many bereaved people of losing a distinct image of their partner's face, or of memories coming when you least expect them, are not uncommon; that folk ideas that have little to do with Christianity can too easily creep unawares into our understanding of heaven.

In addition to these,

- Lewis's book underlines the importance of not just honestly expressing our feelings but *thinking with and through our feelings*. Though for him this took the form of writing, for others it might involve talking to a friend, regular journaling, improvising at the piano, revisiting old places and photographs, or, as was the case with a friend of mine, writ-

90. Beversluis, *Search for Rational Religion*, pp. 156-57.
91. V. Reppert, *C. S. Lewis's Dangerous Idea: In Defense of the Argument from Reason* (Downers Grove, Ill.: InterVarsity Press, 2002), pp. 21-28.
92. Reppert, *C. S. Lewis's Dangerous Idea*, p. 28.

ing poetry — something he had never been able to do before and something he was unable to do afterward.

• Concerning the situation through which our loss has come, we need to be *checking for prior unresolved experiences of pain* that might color and escalate it. We also need to help people move from focusing on intentional memories of the person they have lost, through idealizing or sometimes idolizing them, to being open to reminders of them anywhere and anytime, and ultimately concentrating on their glorified and joy-filled life with God.

• It also involves *delving beneath our confusions or rationalizations,* and allowing our images of how strong our faith is, and of the nature of God himself, to be challenged and at times shattered. For Lewis this entailed moving from feeling God to be at first silent, next cruel, then surgical, to Someone always "there for us" in ways we cannot fully comprehend. For only so can we can we know and be like God more truly. Ultimately, says Lewis, it comes down to what we have always known through Scripture but not fully appropriated in our experience: "Seek first the kingdom of God and his righteousness, and all these things shall be added to you" (Matt. 6:33), leaving the answers to some of our questions about pain and the fulfillment of our deepest longings till we are with God in his coming kingdom.

I began with a description of Joy's funeral and of Lewis's first reactions to it. I would like to conclude with an excerpt from the closing paragraphs of the *The Last Battle,* the final volume in *The Chronicles of Narnia.* This plays a similar part in the series to the closing scenes of the book of Revelation in the Bible, describing as it does the end of Narnia and the beginning of life in Aslan's country.

And soon they found themselves all walking together — and a great, bright possession it was — up towards the mountains higher than you could see in this world even if they were there to be seen. But there was no snow on those mountains: there were forests and green slopes and sweet orchards and flashing waterfalls, one above the other, going up for ever. . . . The light ahead was growing stronger. Lucy saw that a great series of many-coloured cliffs led up in front of them like a giant's staircase. And then she forgot everything else, because Aslan himself was coming, leaping down from cliff to cliff like a living cataract of power and beauty. . . . Then [he] turned to them and said: . . . "Your father and mother and all of you are — as you used to call it in the Shadow-Lands — dead. The term is over: the holidays have begun. The dream is ended: this is the morning." And as He spoke He no longer looked to them like a lion; but the things that began to happen after that were so great and beautiful that I cannot write them. And for us this is the end of all the stories, and we can most truly say that they all lived happily ever after. But for them it was only the beginning of the real story. And their life in this world and their adventures in Narnia had only been the cover and the title page: now at last they were beginning Chapter One of the Great Story, which no one on earth has read: which goes on for ever: in which every chapter is better than the one before.[93]

93. C. S. Lewis, *The Last Battle* (London: Bodley Head, 1955), pp. 164-65.

Contributors

GWENFAIR WALTERS ADAMS is Associate Professor of Church History at Gordon-Conwell Theological Seminary, South Hamilton, Massachusetts, and is the author of *Visions in Late Medieval England: Lay Spirituality and Sacred Glimpses of the Hidden Worlds of Faith* (E. J. Brill, 2007).

ROBERT BANKS, formerly Professor of the Ministry of the Laity and Chair of the Ministry Division at Fuller Theological Seminary, Pasadena, California, is currently an Associate of the Centre for the History of Christian Thought & Experience, School of Humanities, Macquarie University, Sydney, and is the author of *Re-Envisioning Theological Education: A Missional Alternative to Current Approaches* (Eerdmans, 1999).

PETER G. BOLT is Head of New Testament Studies at Moore Theological College, Sydney, and is the author of *The Cross from a Distance: Atonement in Mark's Gospel* (InterVarsity Press, 2005).

ANDREW CAMERON lectures in Ethics at Moore Theological College, Sydney, and is the co-editor (with Brian Rosner) of *Still Deadly: Ancient Cures for the Seven Sins* (Aquila Press, 2007).

RICHARD GIBSON lectures in New Testament, Church History, and Greek at Moore Theological College, Sydney, and edited *Interpreting God's Plan: Biblical Theology and the Pastor* (Paternoster, 1998).

Brian S. Rosner is Faculty Research Advisor and lectures in New Testament and Ethics at Moore Theological College, Sydney, and is the author of *Greed as Idolatry: The Origin and Meaning of a Pauline Metaphor* (Eerdmans, 2007).

Mark D. Thompson is Head of Theology and Academic Dean, Moore Theological College, Sydney, and is the author of *A Clear and Present Word: The Clarity of Scripture* (InterVarsity Press, 2006).